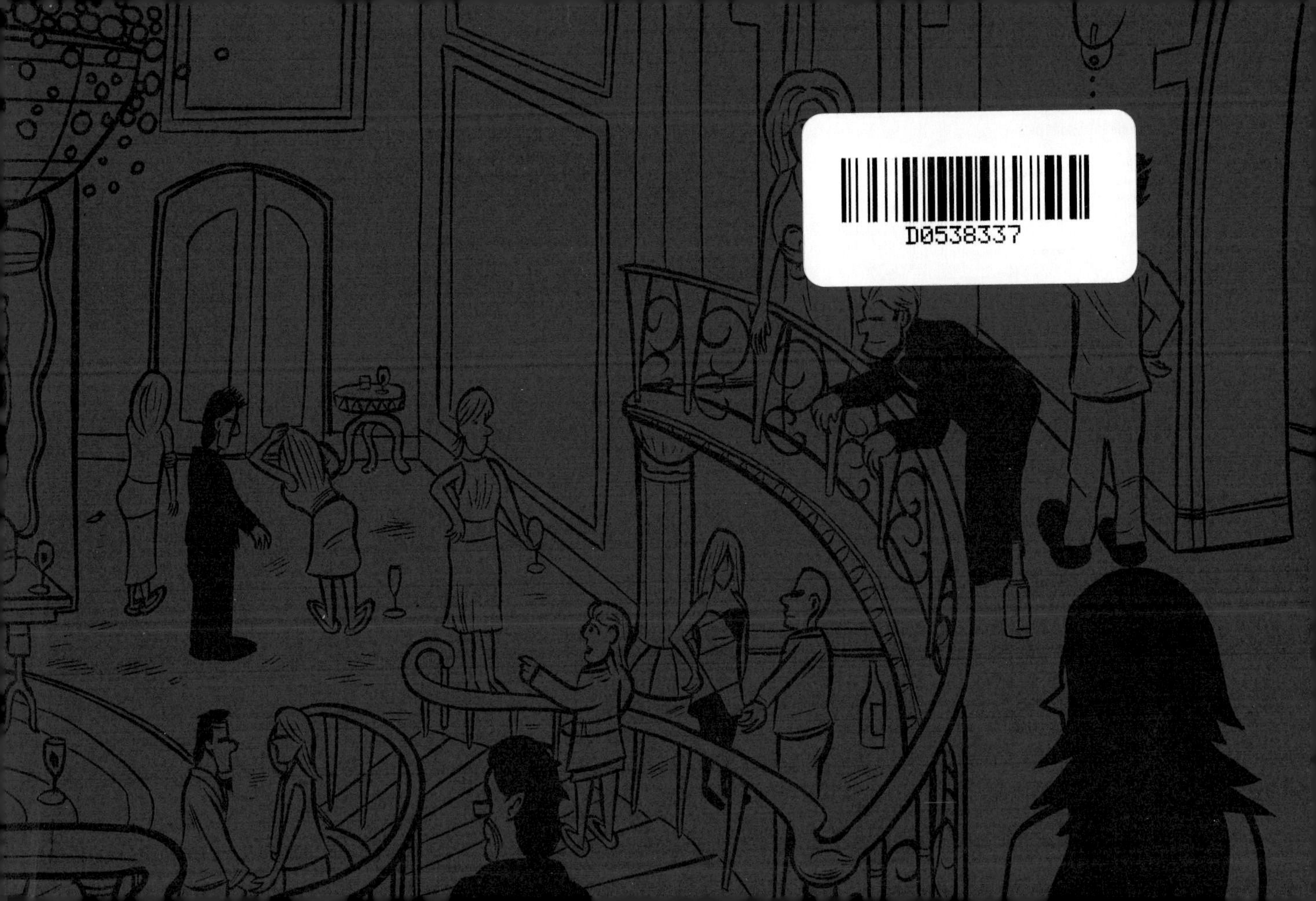

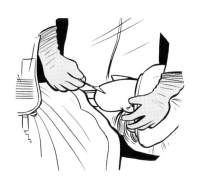

Fingerprints © 2010 Will Dinski

ISBN 978 - 1 - 60309 - 053 - 7

1. Graphic Novels

2. Cosmetic Surgery

3. Celebrity Culture

Top Shelf Productions

P.O. Box 1282

Marietta, Georgia

30061-1282

The United States of America

WWW. topshelfcomix.com

WWW. willdinski.com

Published by Top Shelf Productions, Inc.

Publishers: Brett Warnock and Chris Staros

Book Design: Will Dinski

First Printing, 2010

Printed in China

WILL DINSKI
MINNEAPOLIS, MINNESOTA

Fingerprints

TOP SHELF PRODUCTIONS
ATLANTA · PORTLAND

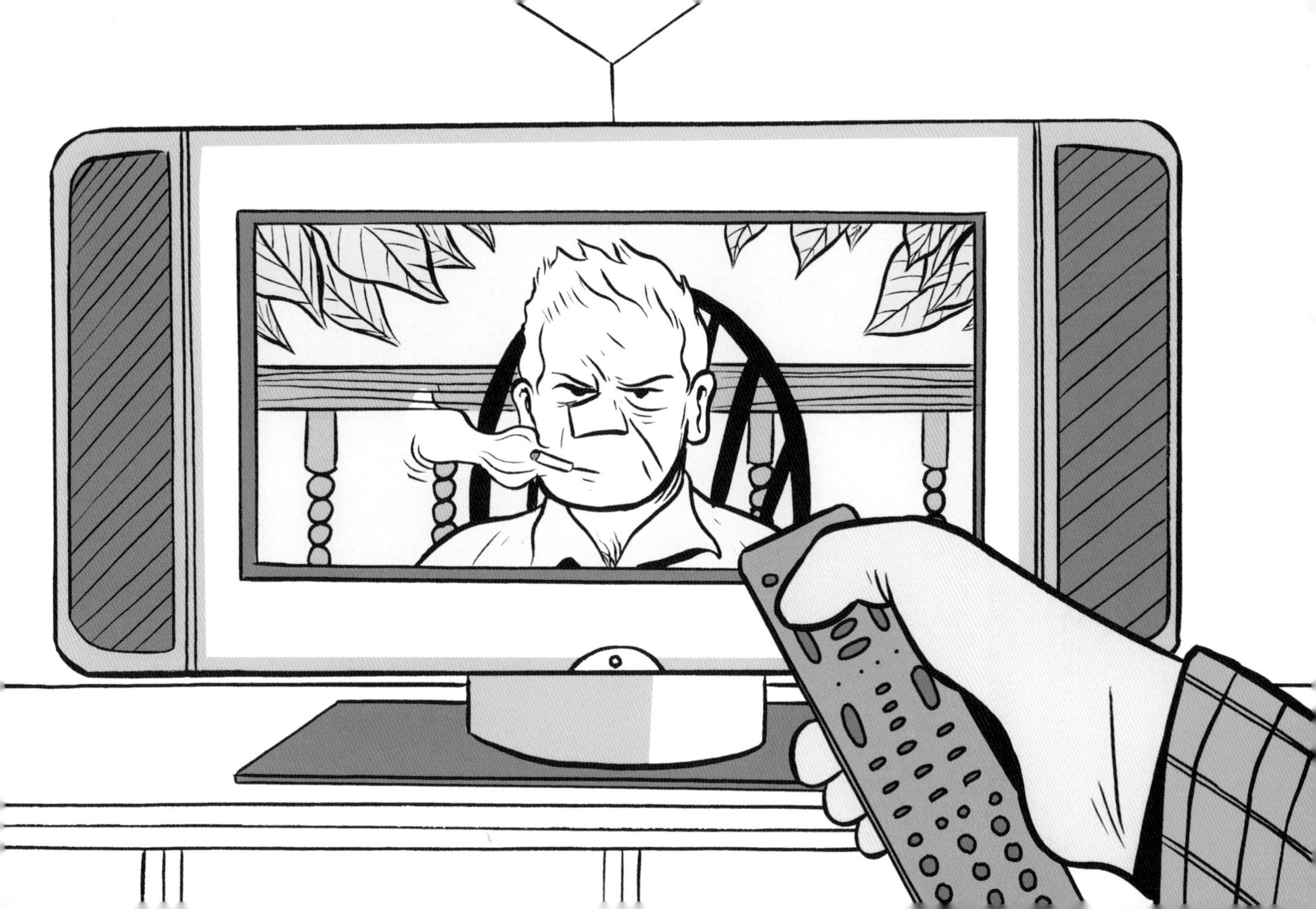

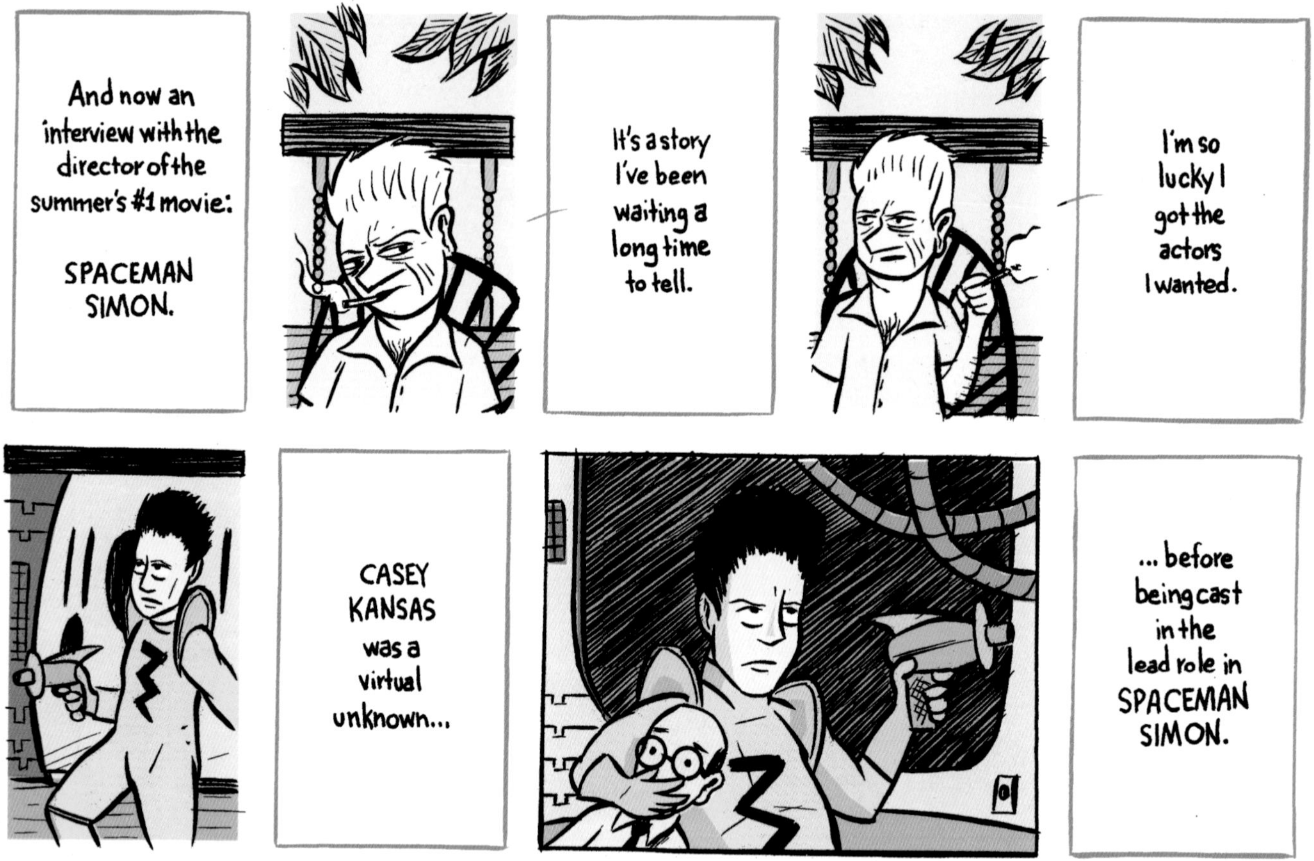
And now an interview with the director of the summer's #1 movie:
SPACEMAN SIMON.
It's a story I've been waiting a long time to tell.
I'm so lucky I got the actors I wanted.
CASEY KANSAS was a virtual unknown...
... before being cast in the lead role in SPACEMAN SIMON.

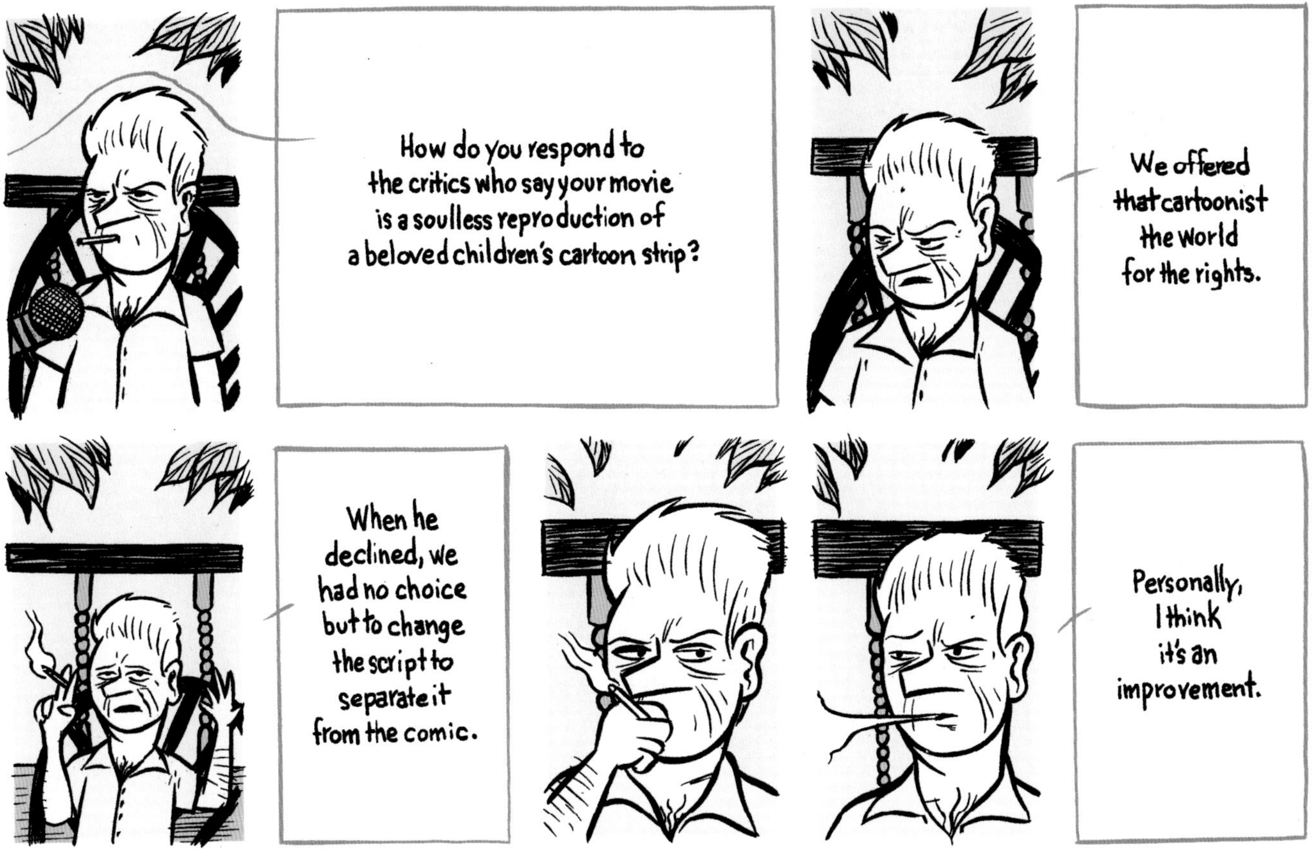
How do you respond to the critics who say your movie is a soulless reproduction of a beloved children's cartoon strip?
We offered that cartoonist the world for the rights.
When he declined, we had no choice but to change the script to separate it from the comic.
Personally, I think it's an improvement.

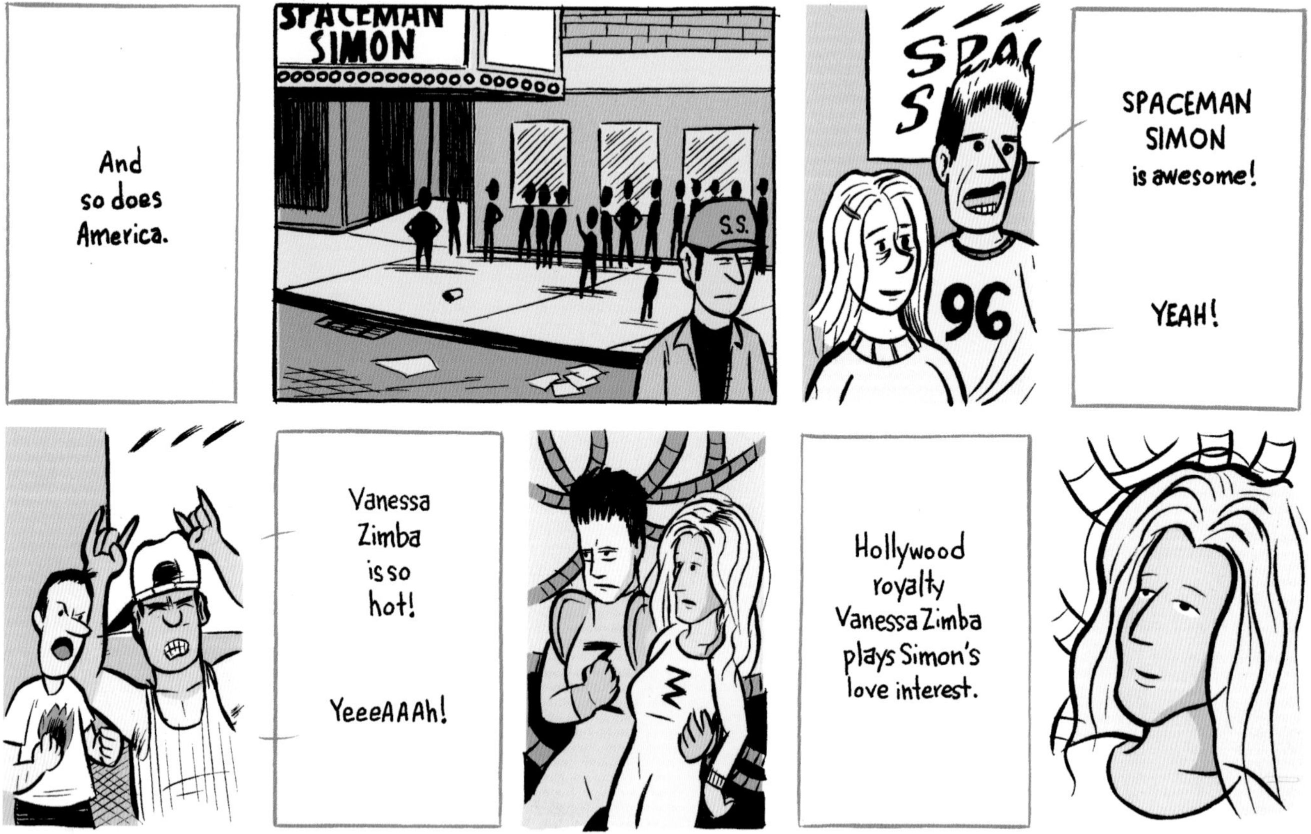
And so does America.
SPACEMAN SIMON
S.S.
96
SPACEMAN SIMON is awesome!
YEAH!
Vanessa Zimba is so hot!
YeeeAAAh!
Hollywood royalty Vanessa Zimba plays Simon's love interest.

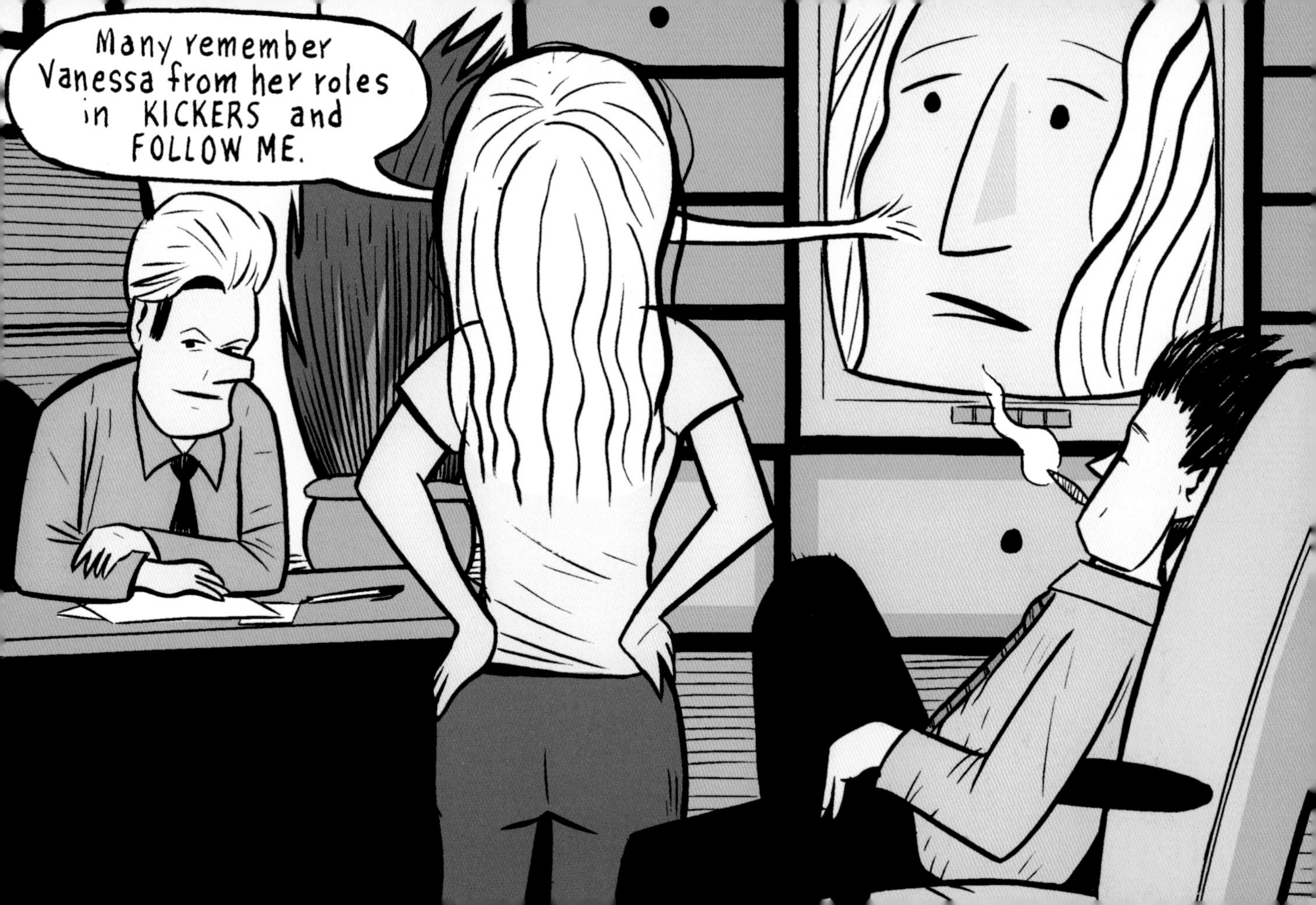
Many remember Vanessa from her roles in KICKERS and FOLLOW ME.

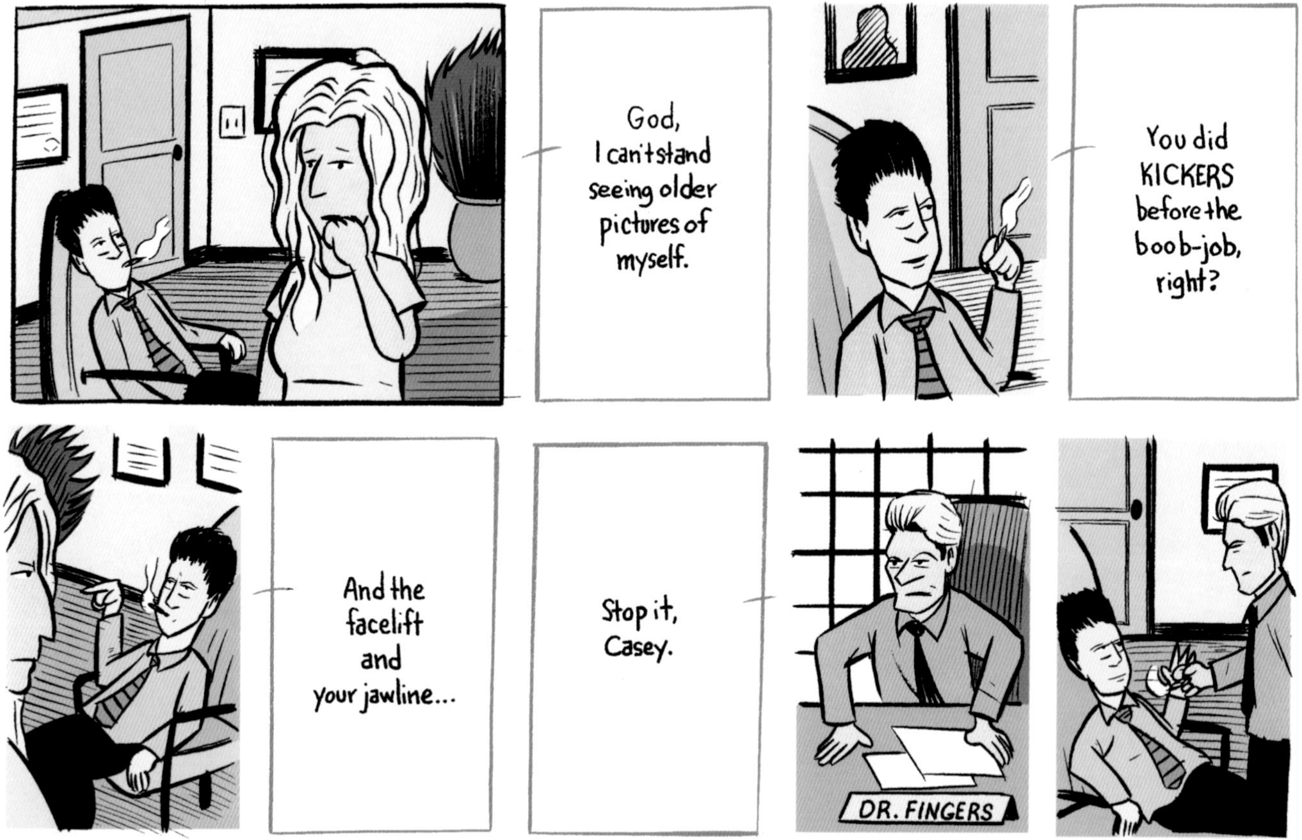
God, I can't stand seeing older pictures of myself.
You did KICKERS before the boob-job, right?
And the facelift and your jawline...
Stop it, Casey.
DR. FINGERS

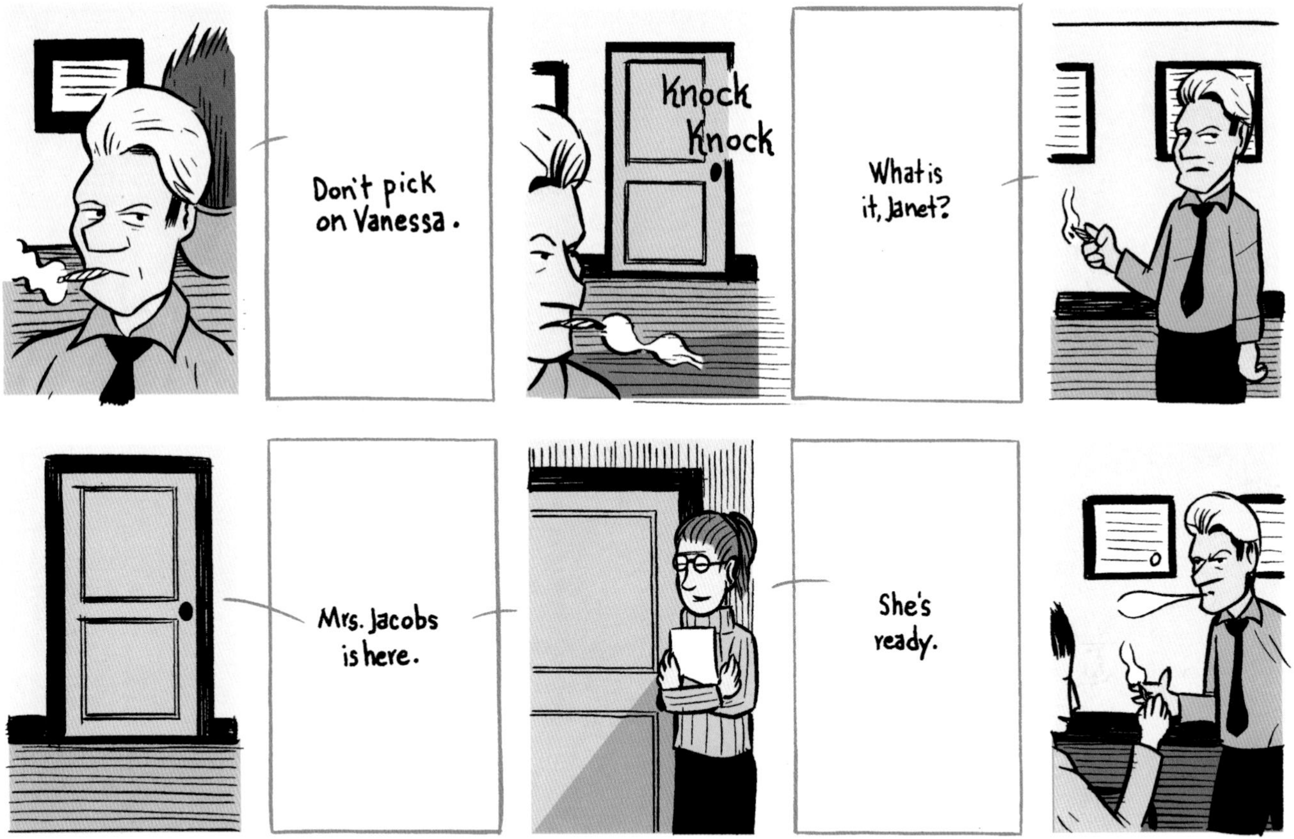
Don't pick on Vanessa.
Knock Knock
What is it, Janet?
Mrs. Jacobs is here.
She's ready.

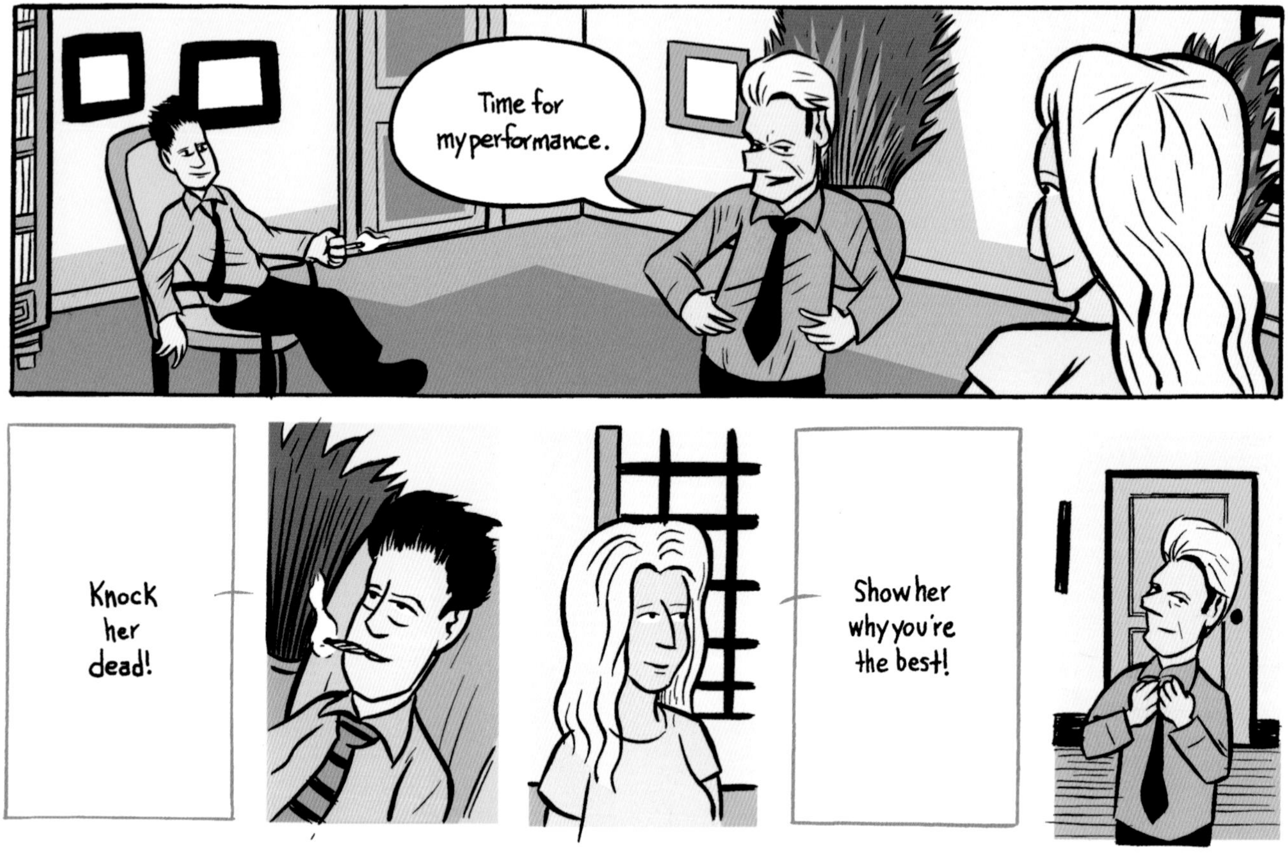
Time for my performance.
Knock her dead!
Show her why you're the best!

Is she prepped?

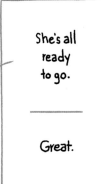

She's all ready to go.

———

Great.

Hello, Muriel.

———

Dr. Fingers!

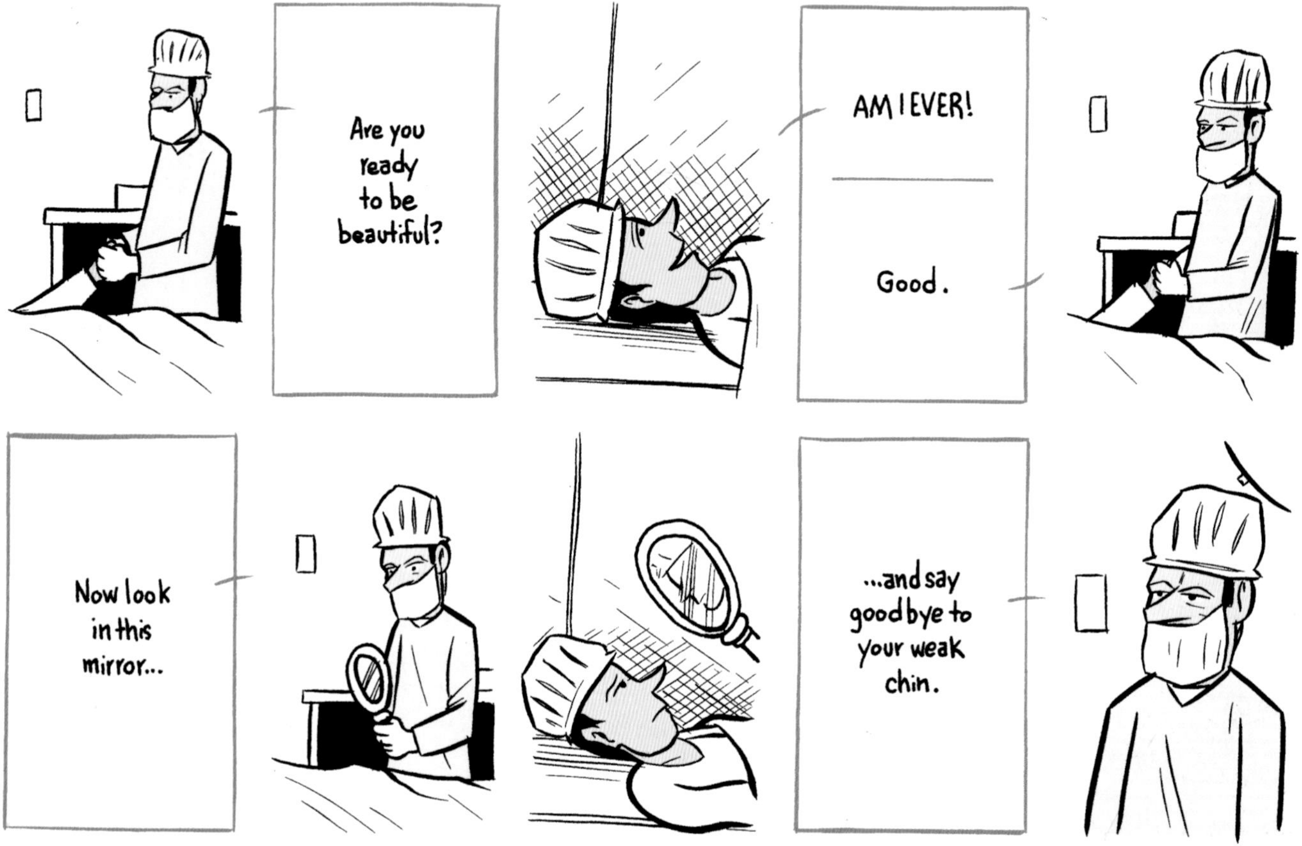
Are you ready to be beautiful?
AM I EVER!
Good.
Now look in this mirror...
...and say goodbye to your weak chin.

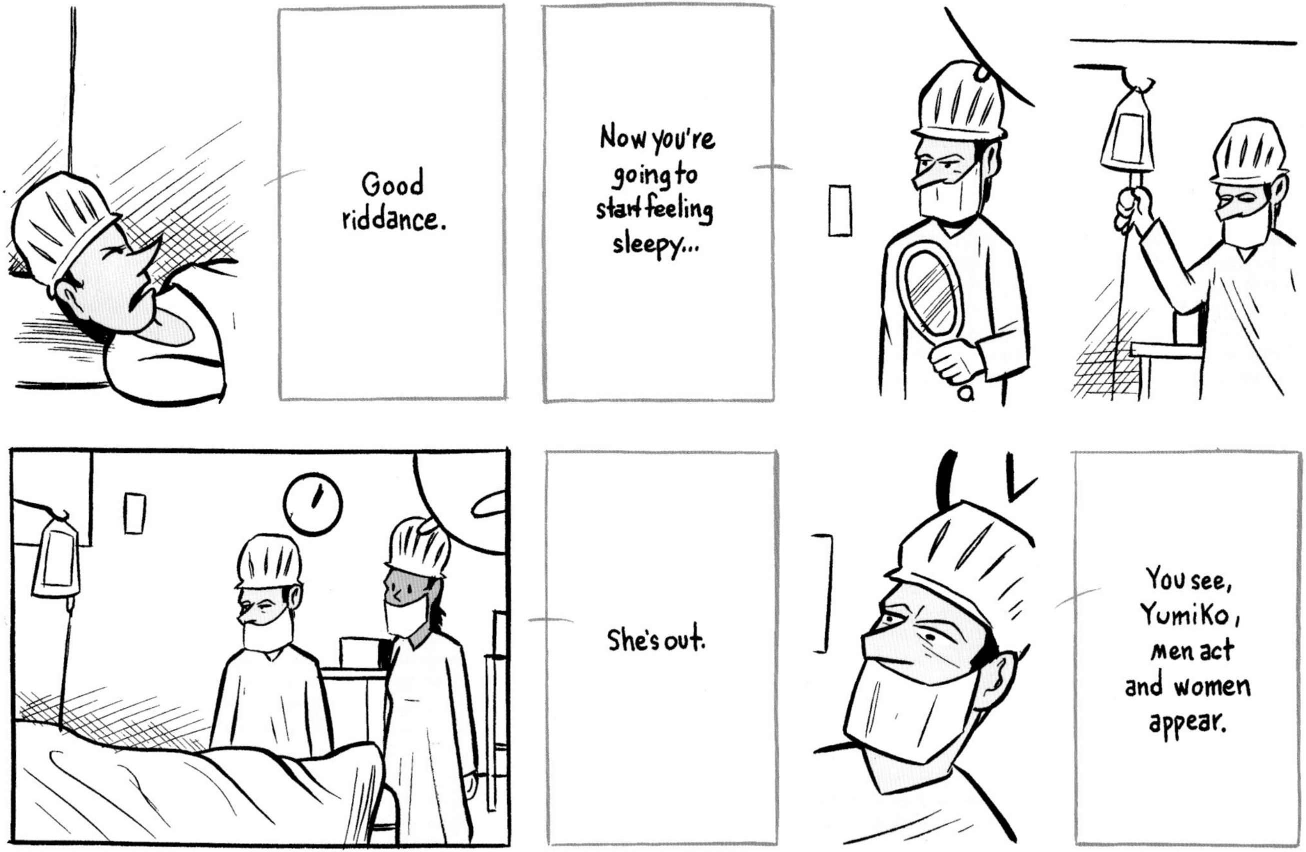

Good riddance.
Now you're going to start feeling sleepy...
She's out.
You see, Yumiko, men act and women appear.

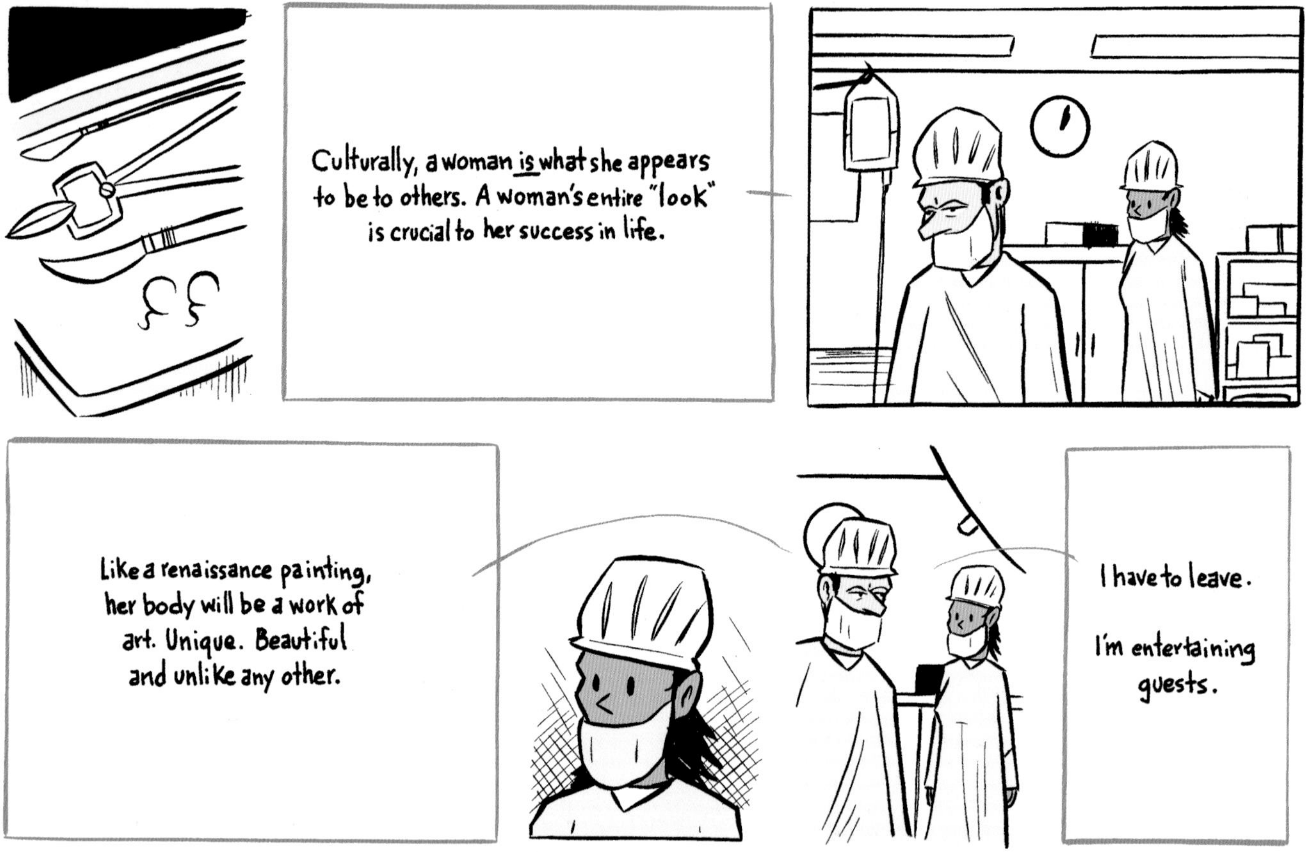
Culturally, a woman is what she appears to be to others. A woman's entire "look" is crucial to her success in life.
Like a renaissance painting, her body will be a work of art. Unique. Beautiful and unlike any other.
I have to leave.
I'm entertaining guests.

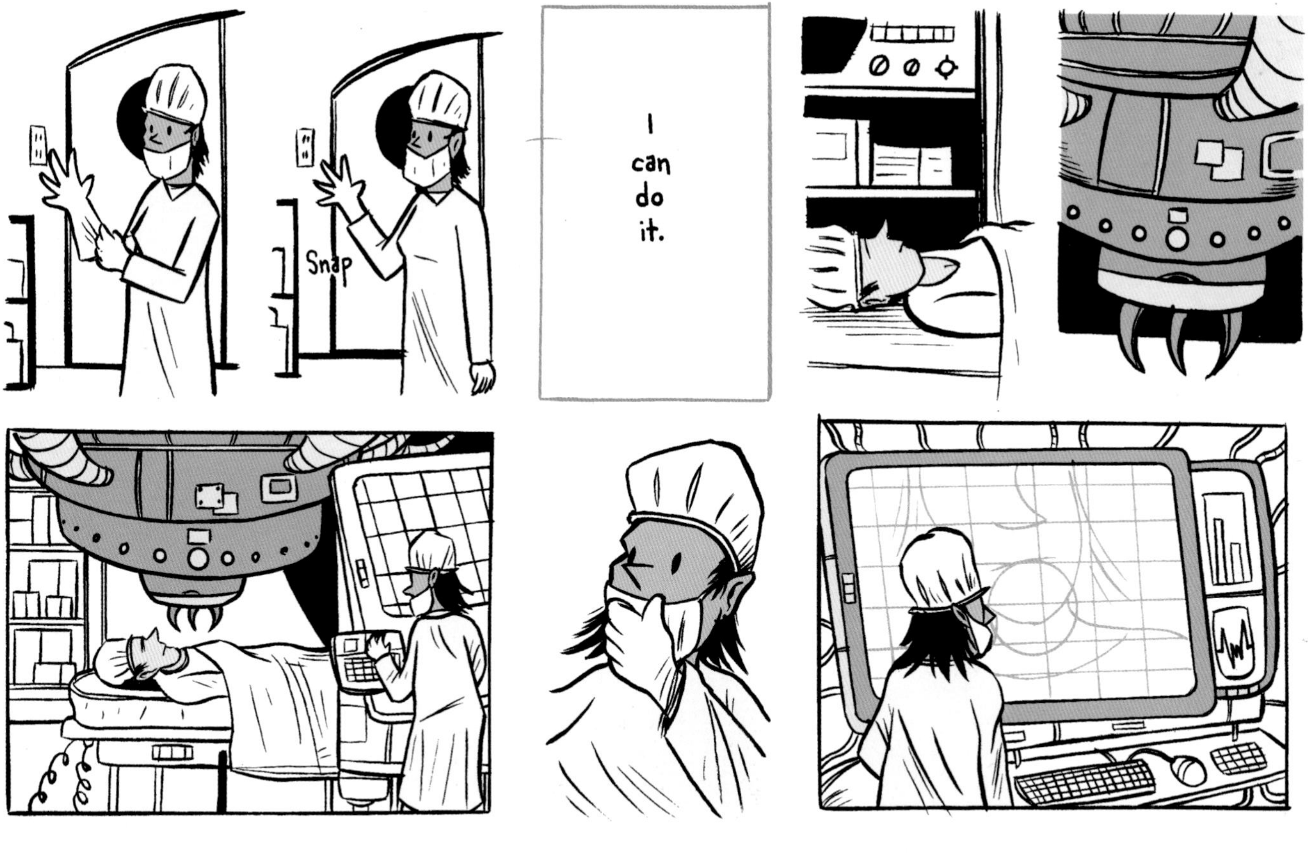
Snap
I can do it.

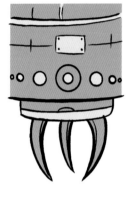

What's this?

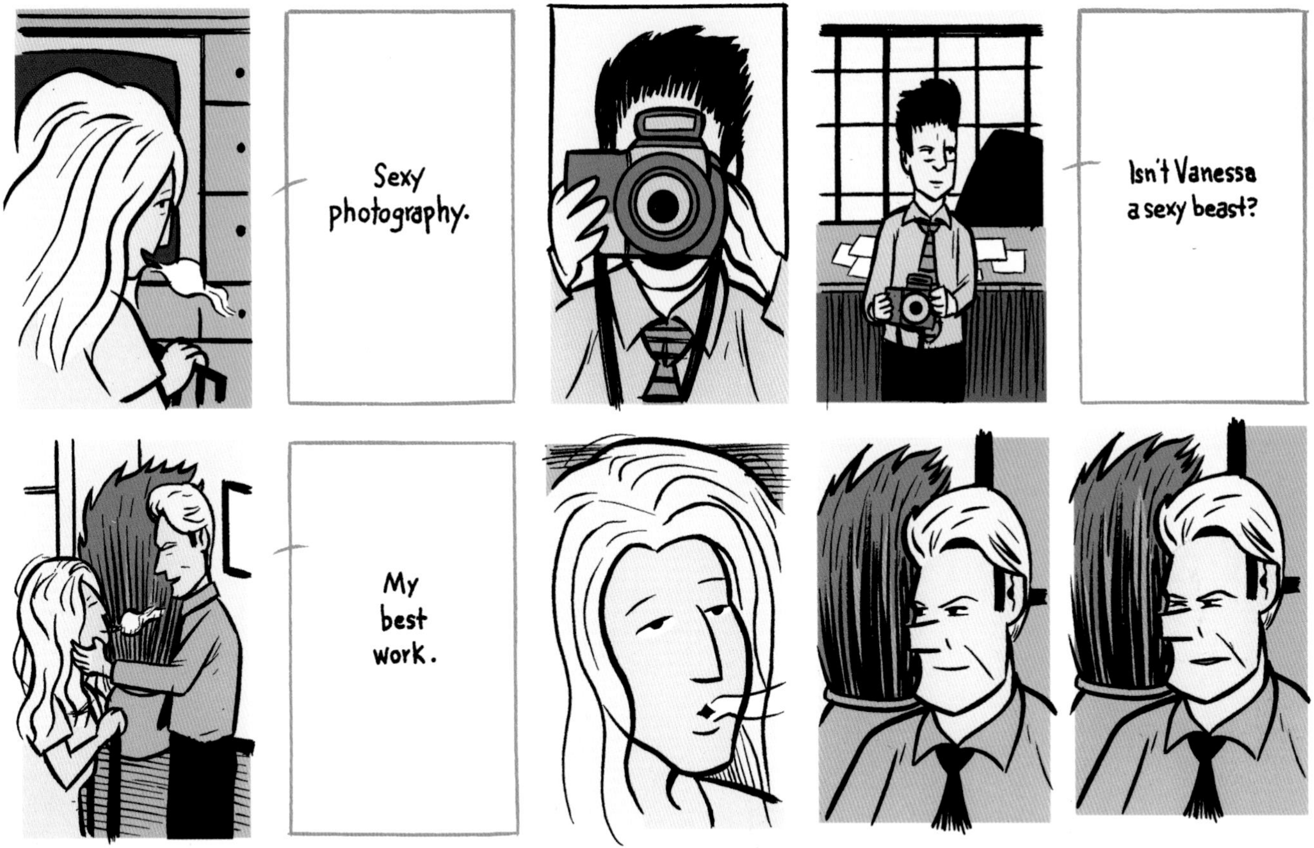
Sexy photography.
Isn't Vanessa a sexy beast?
My best work.

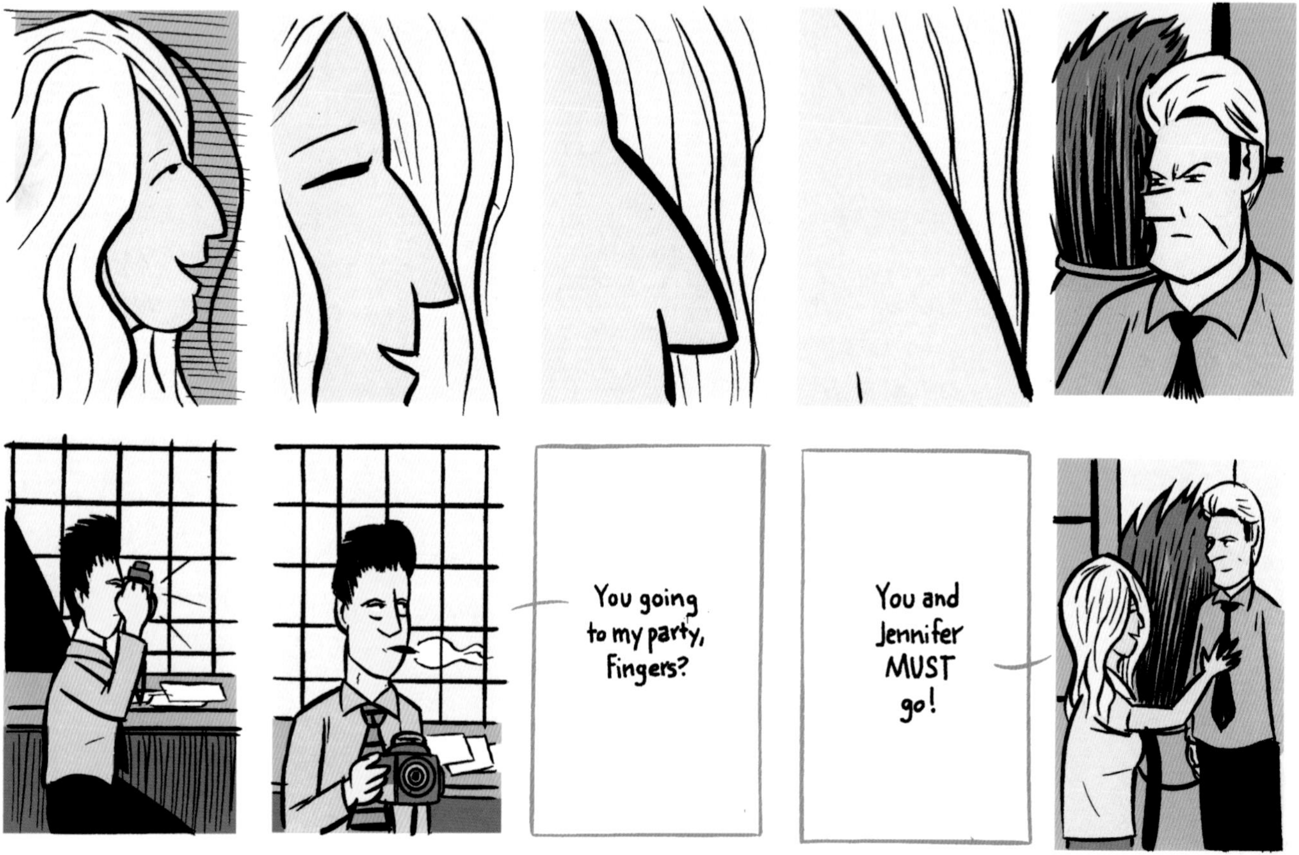
You going to my party, Fingers?
You and Jennifer MUST go!

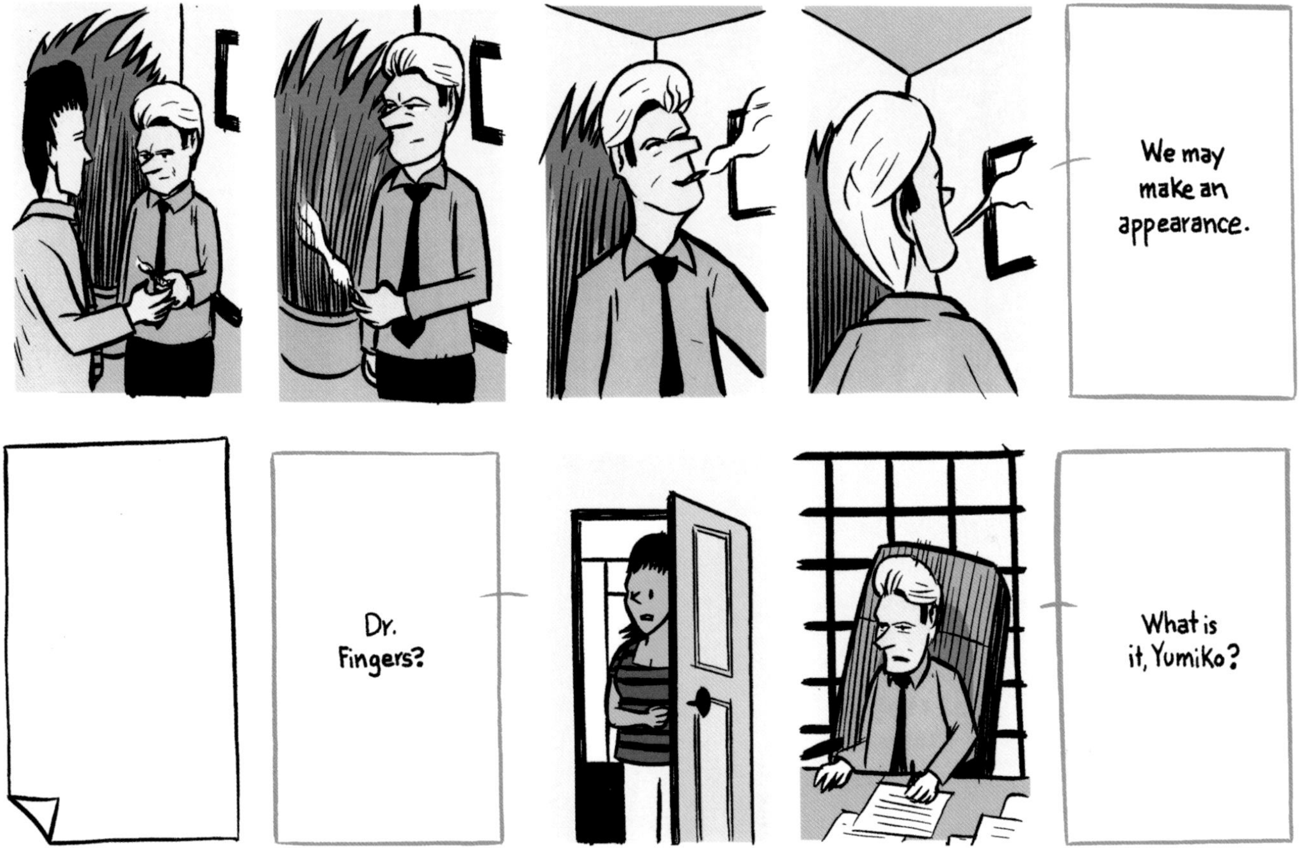
We may make an appearance.
Dr. Fingers?
What is it, Yumiko?

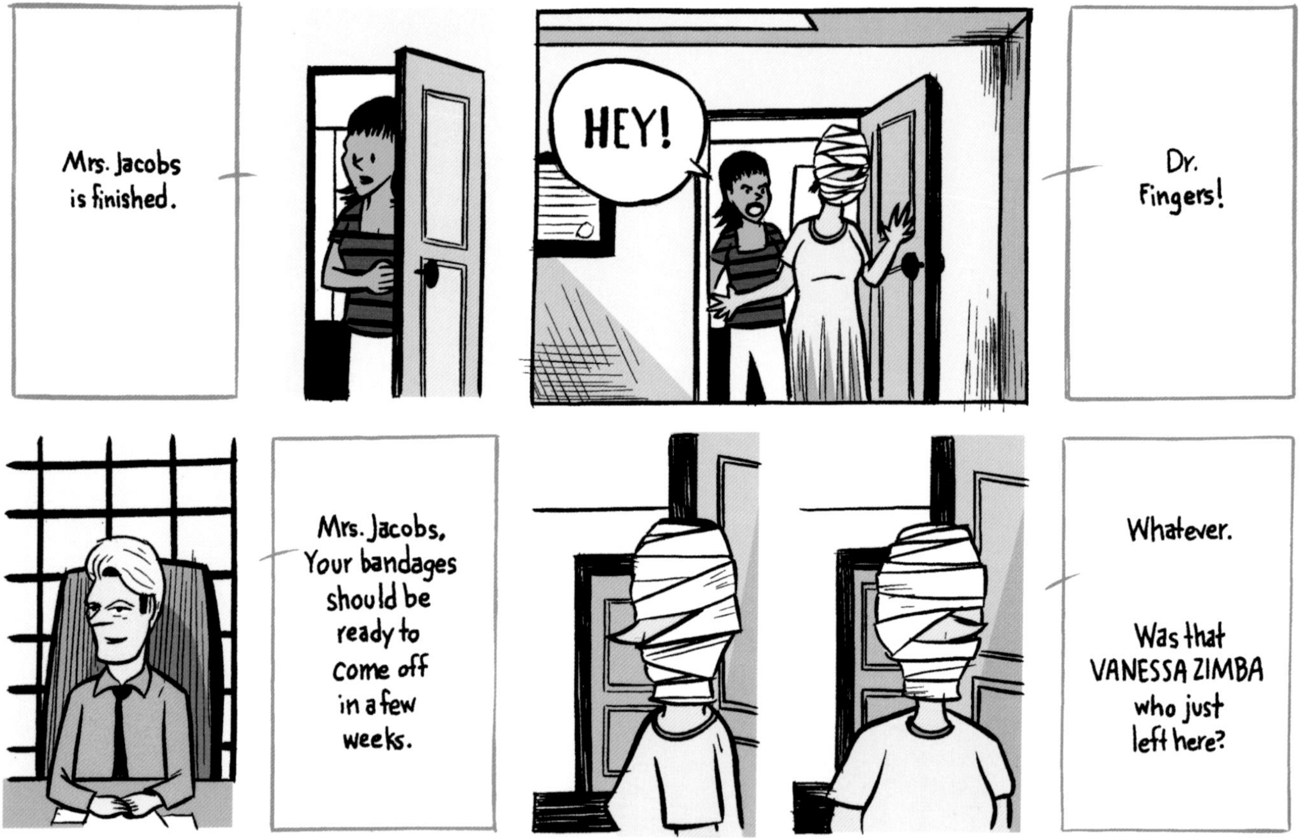
Mrs. Jacobs is finished.
HEY!
Dr. Fingers!
Mrs. Jacobs, Your bandages should be ready to come off in a few weeks.
Whatever.
Was that VANESSA ZIMBA who just left here?

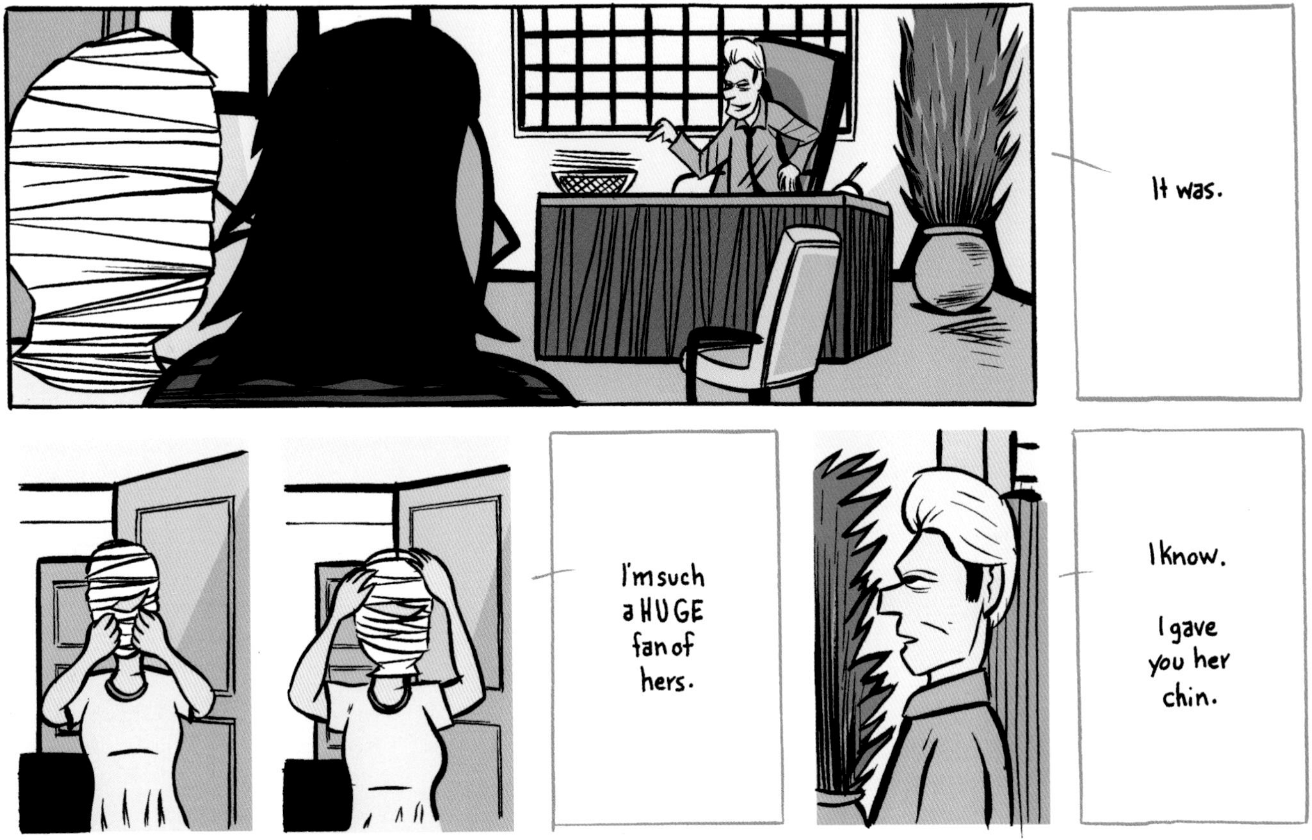
It was.
I'm such a HUGE fan of hers.
I know.
I gave you her chin.

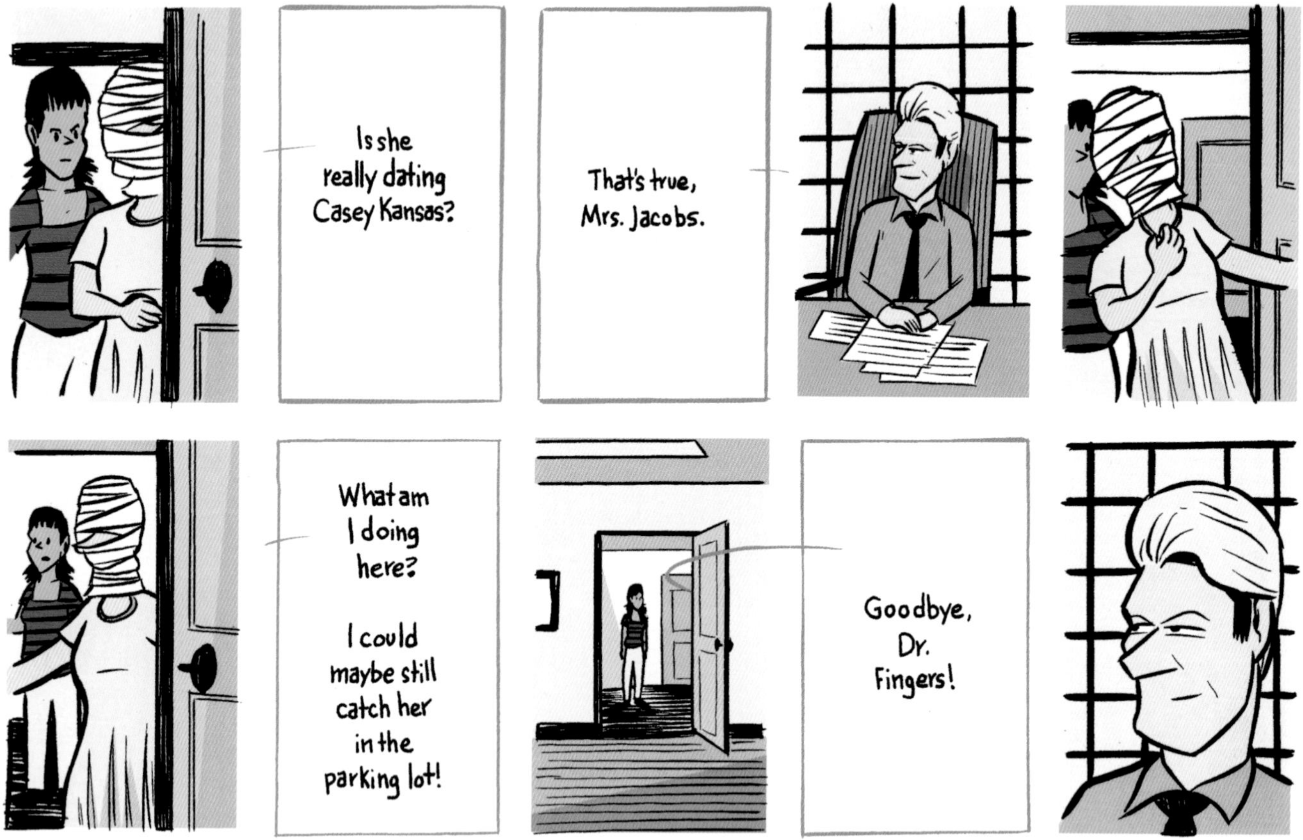

Is she really dating Casey Kansas?
That's true, Mrs. Jacobs.
What am I doing here?
I could maybe still catch her in the parking lot!
Goodbye, Dr. Fingers!

I didn't know Vanessa was dating Casey.

She isn't.

It's just a stunt for the tabloids.

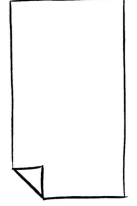

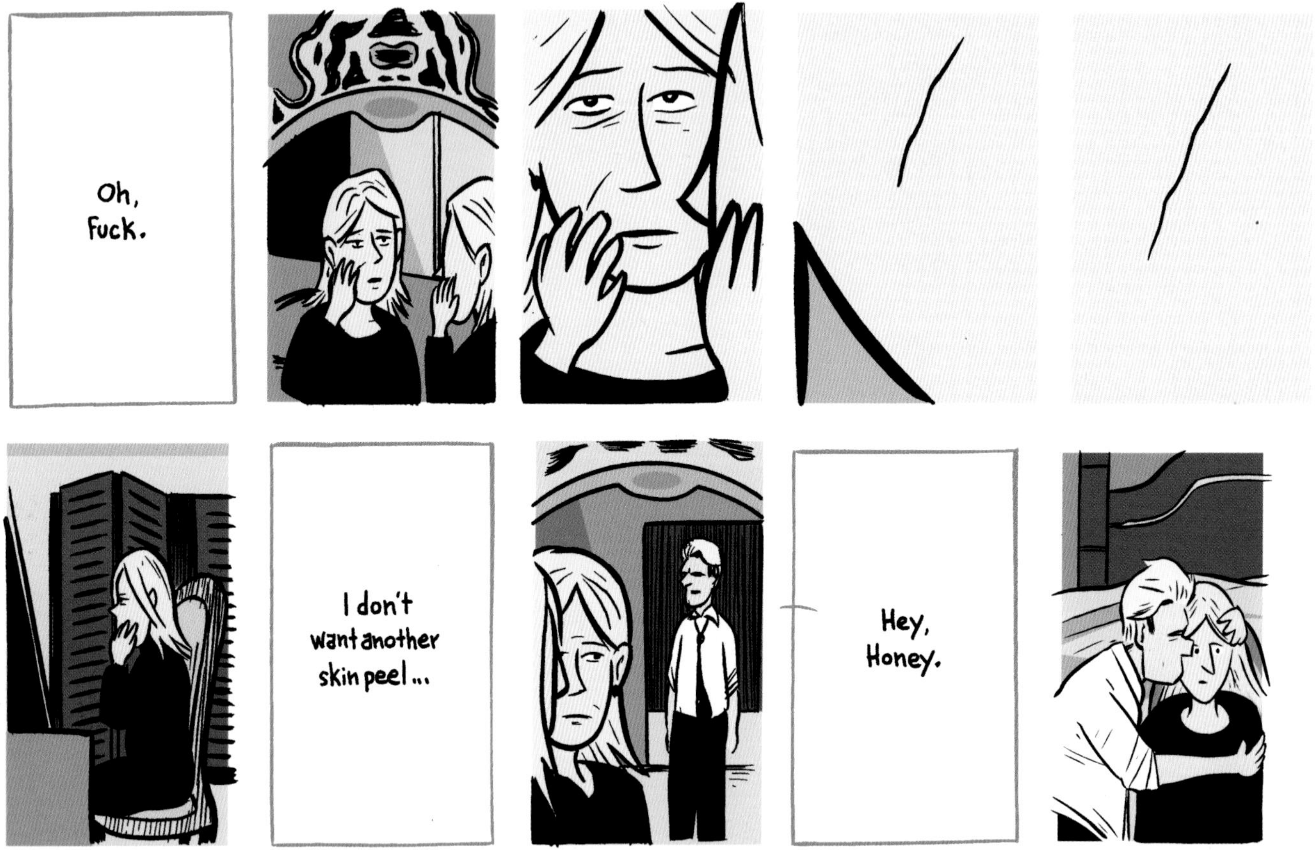
Oh, Fuck.
I don't want another skin peel...
Hey, Honey.

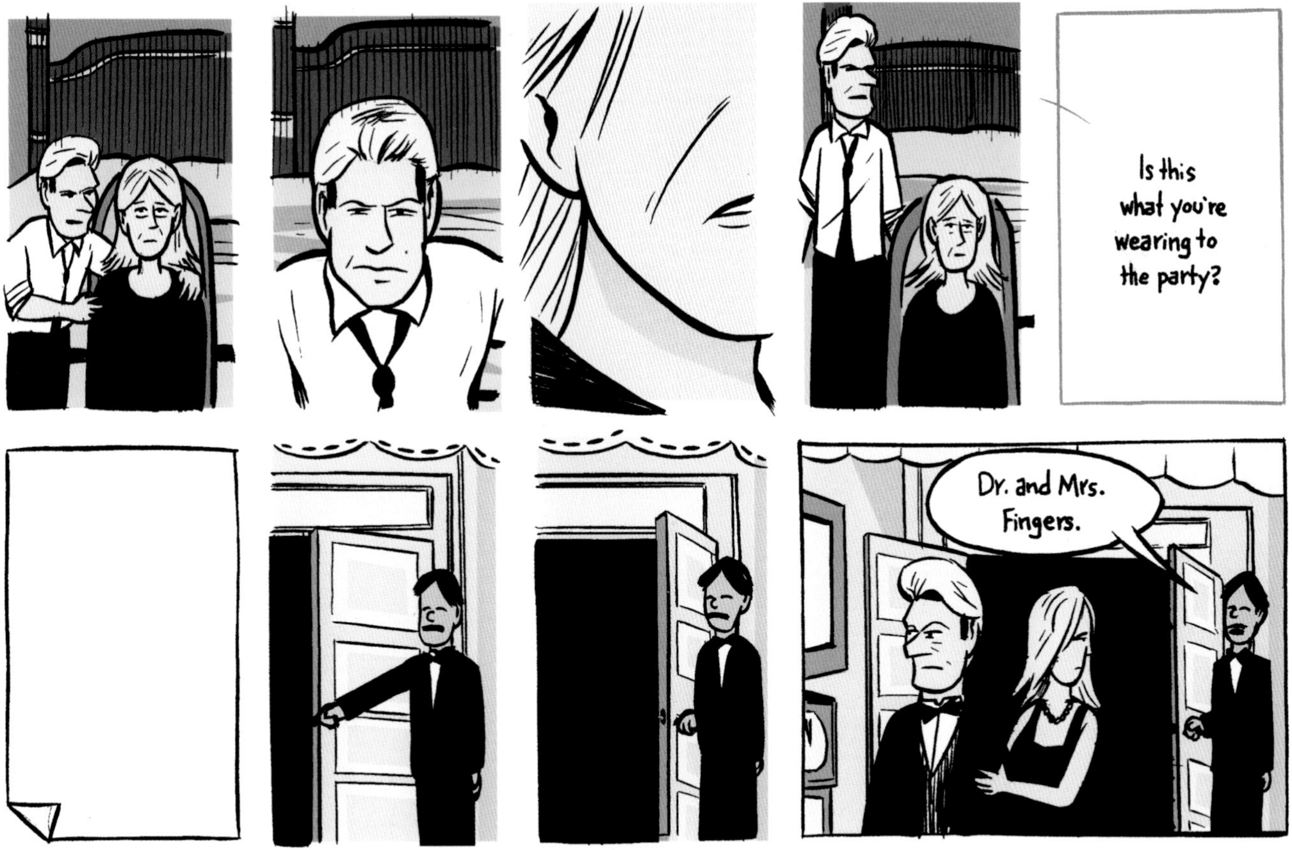
Is this what you're wearing to the party?
Dr. and Mrs. Fingers.

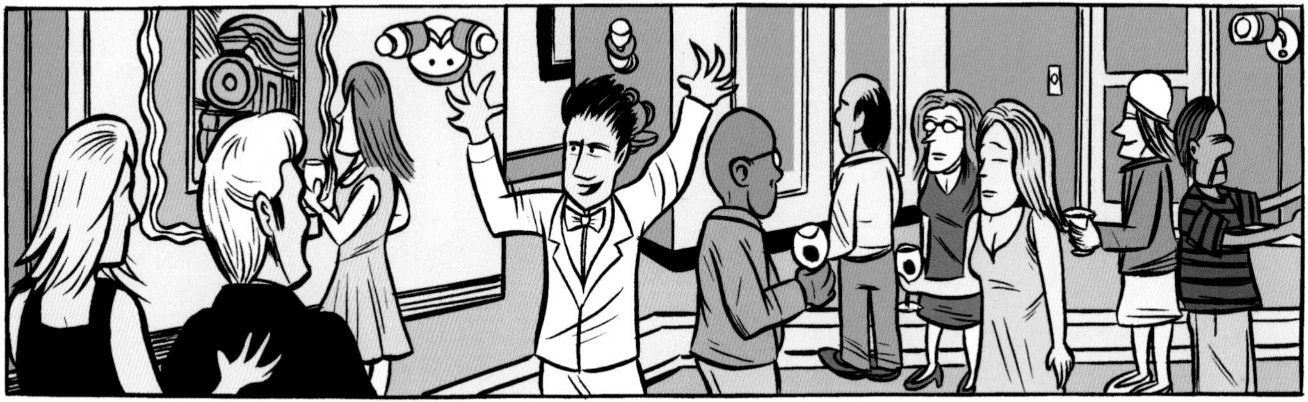

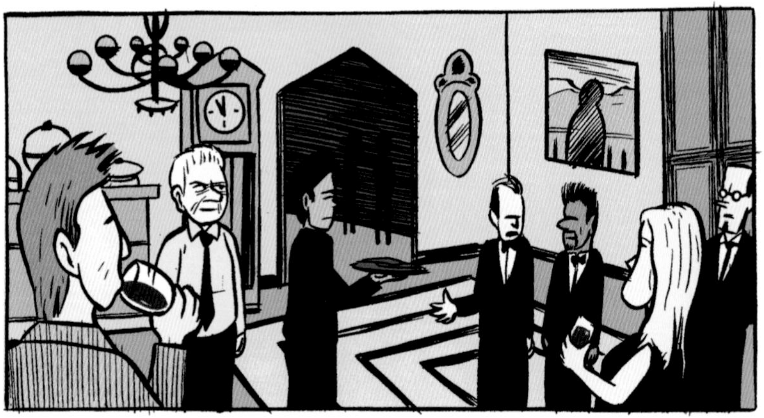

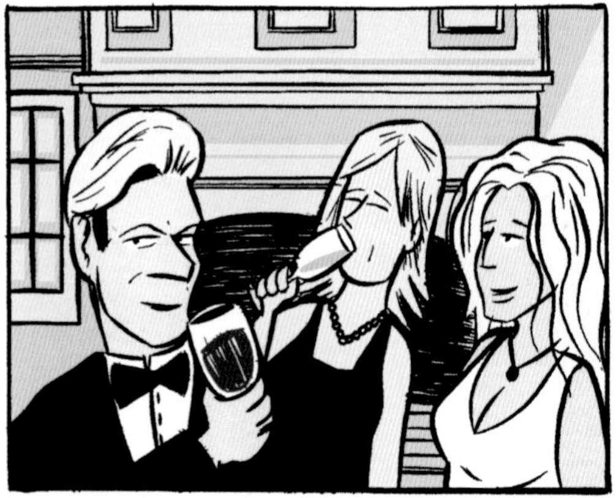

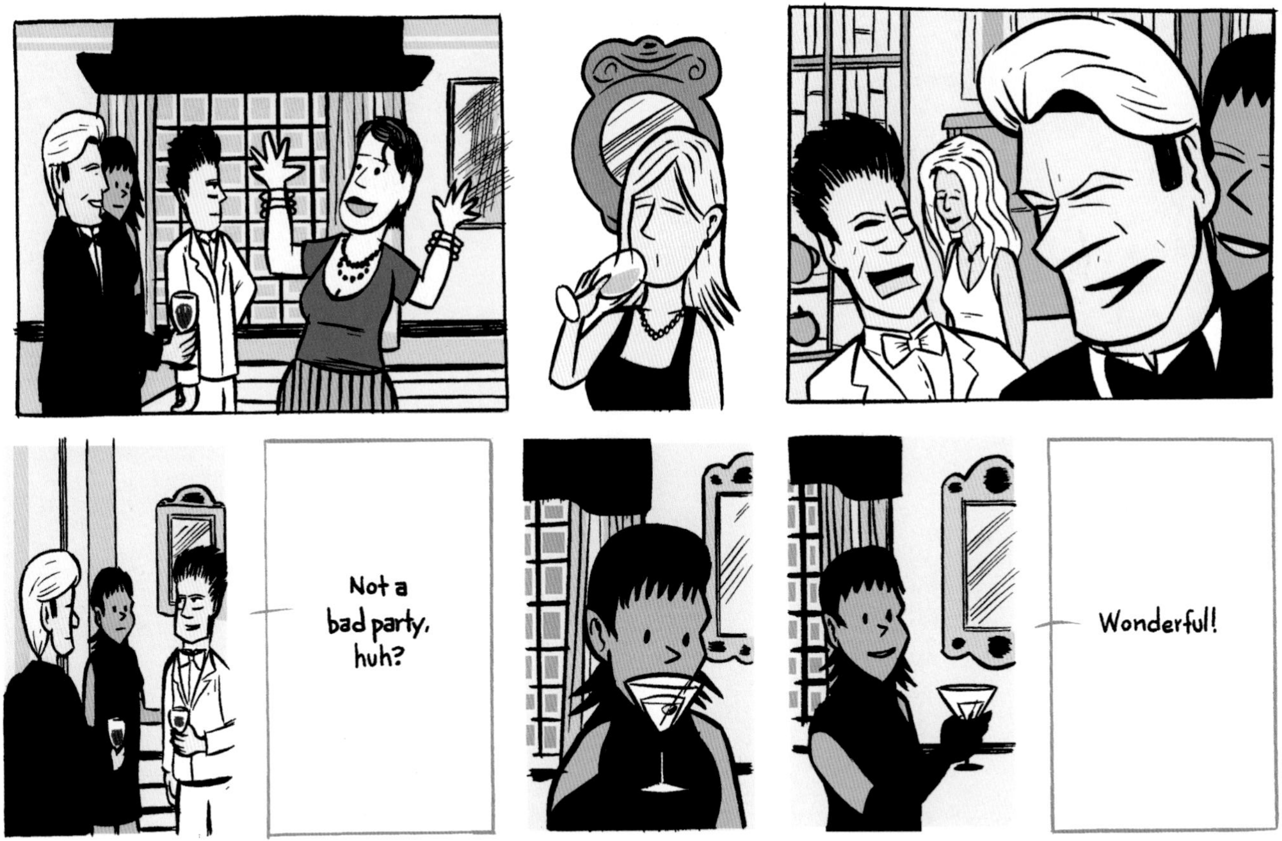
Not a
bad party,
huh?
Wonderful!

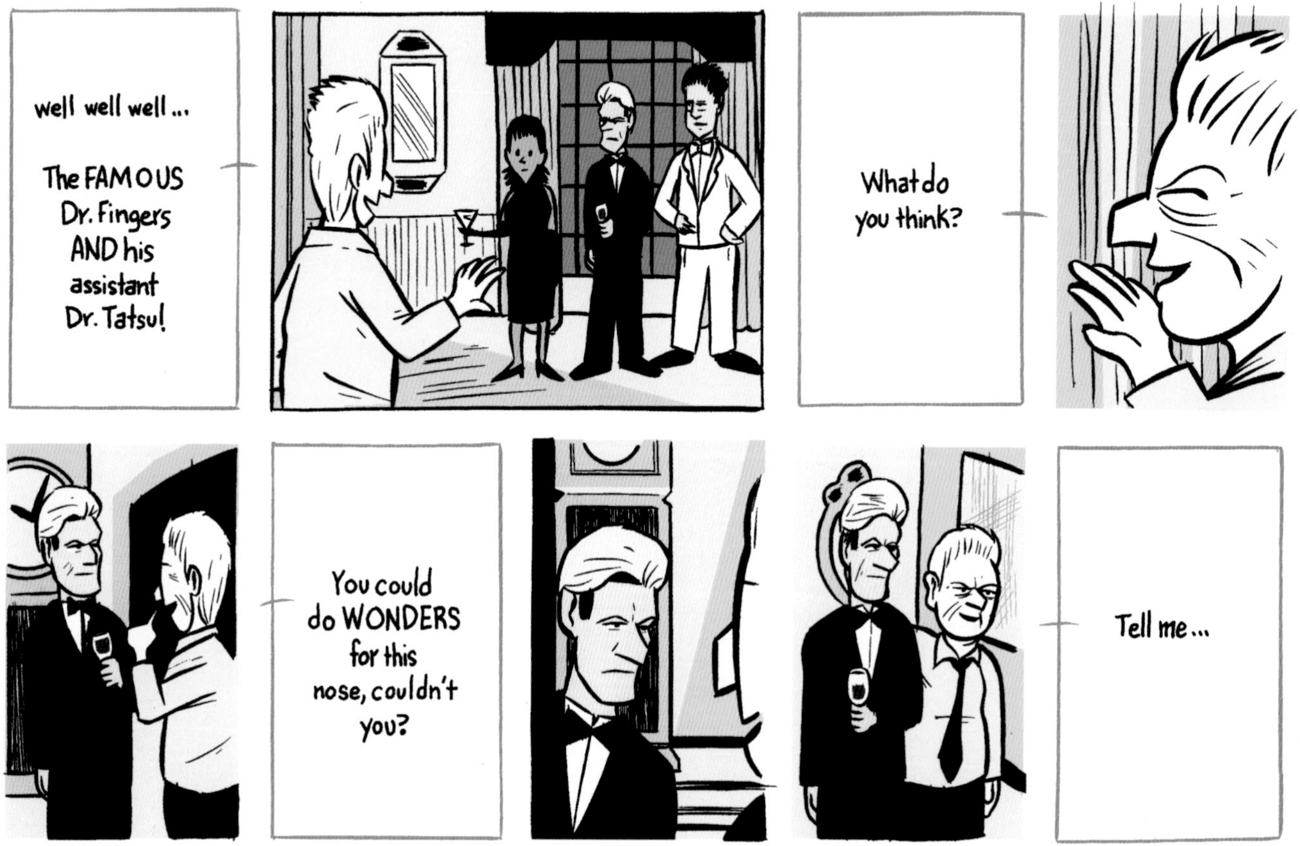
well well well ...
The FAMOUS Dr. Fingers AND his assistant Dr. Tatsu!
What do you think?
You could do WONDERS for this nose, couldn't you?
Tell me ...

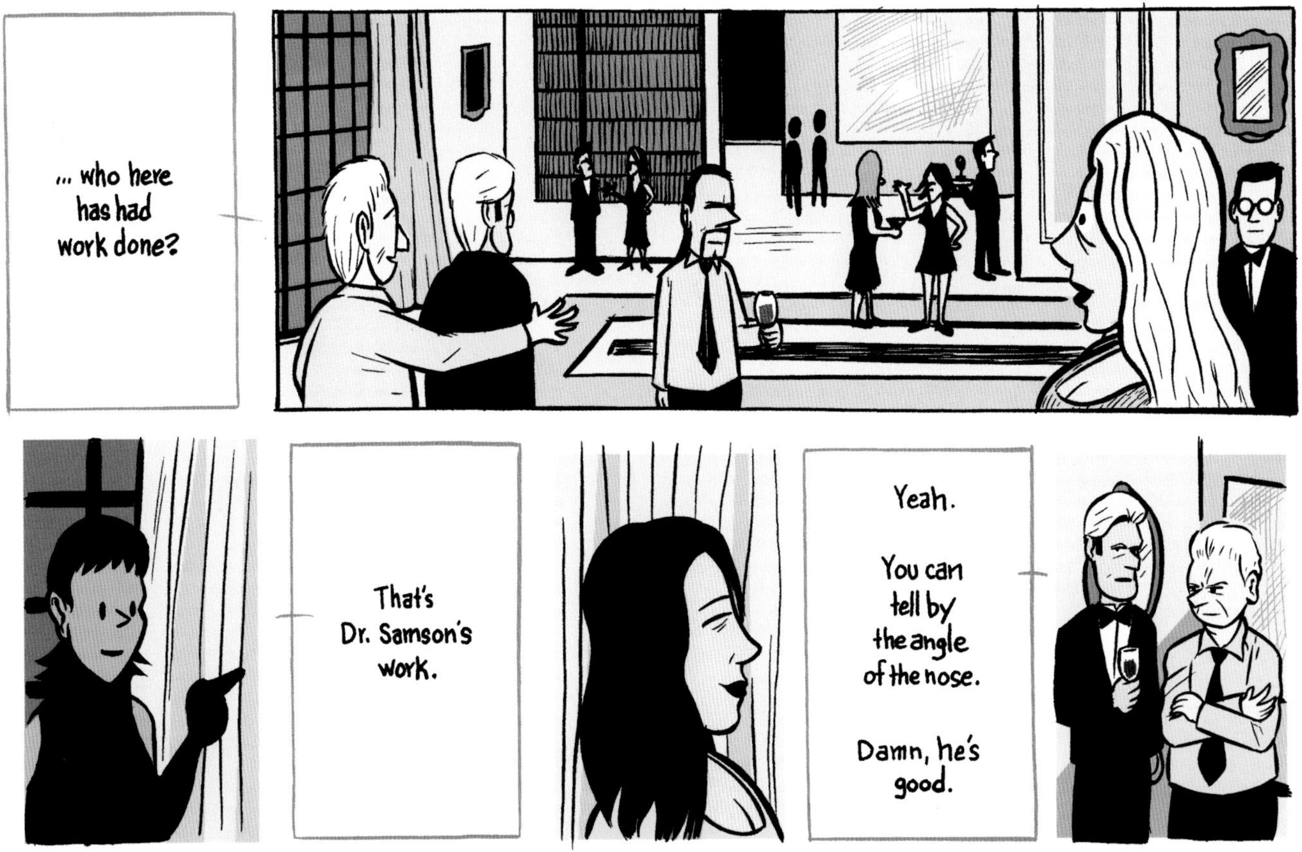
... who here has had work done?
That's Dr. Samson's work.
Yeah.
You can tell by the angle of the nose.
Damn, he's good.

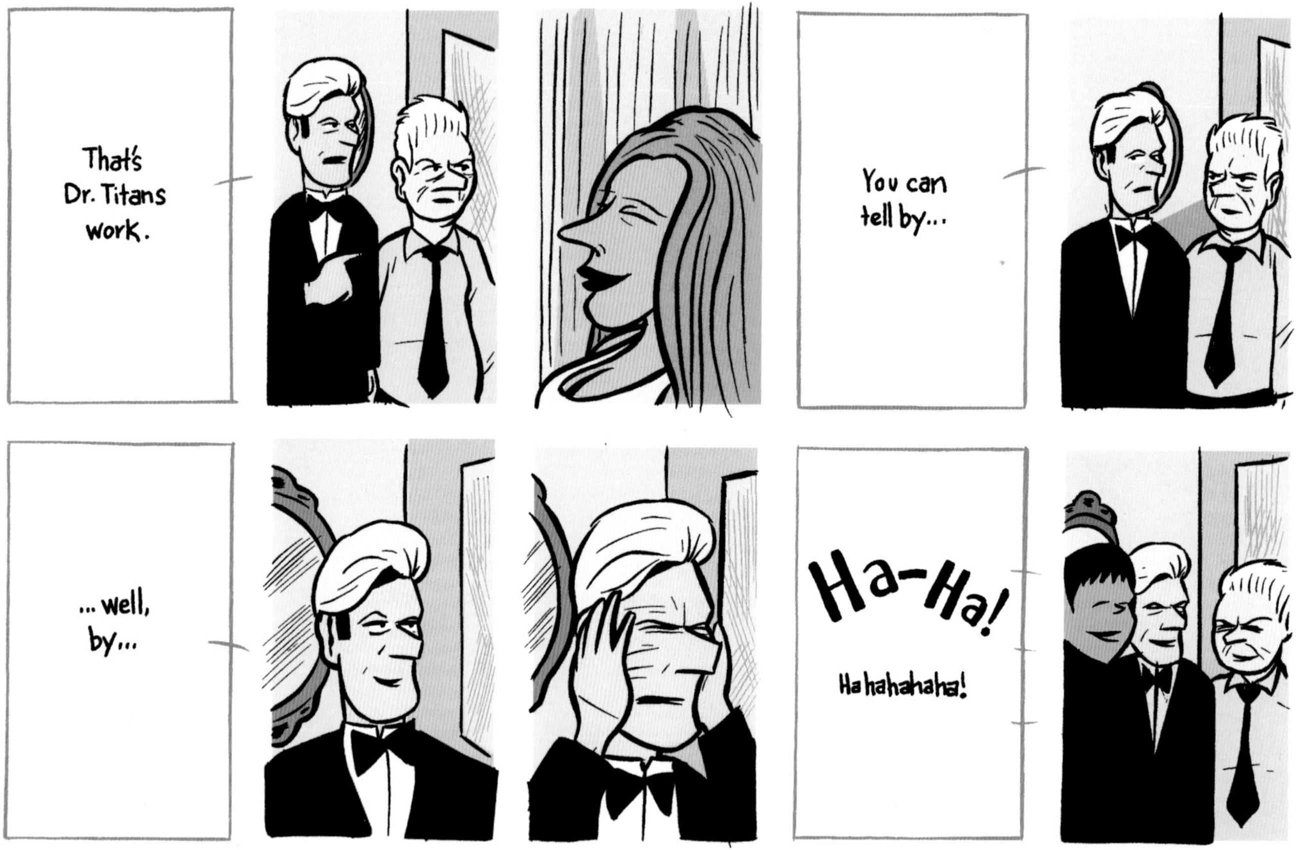
That's Dr. Titans work.
You can tell by...
... well, by...
Ha-Ha!
Ha hahahaha!

... I'll bet my pal fingers could take ...

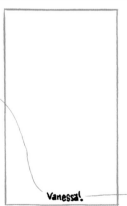

Vanessa!

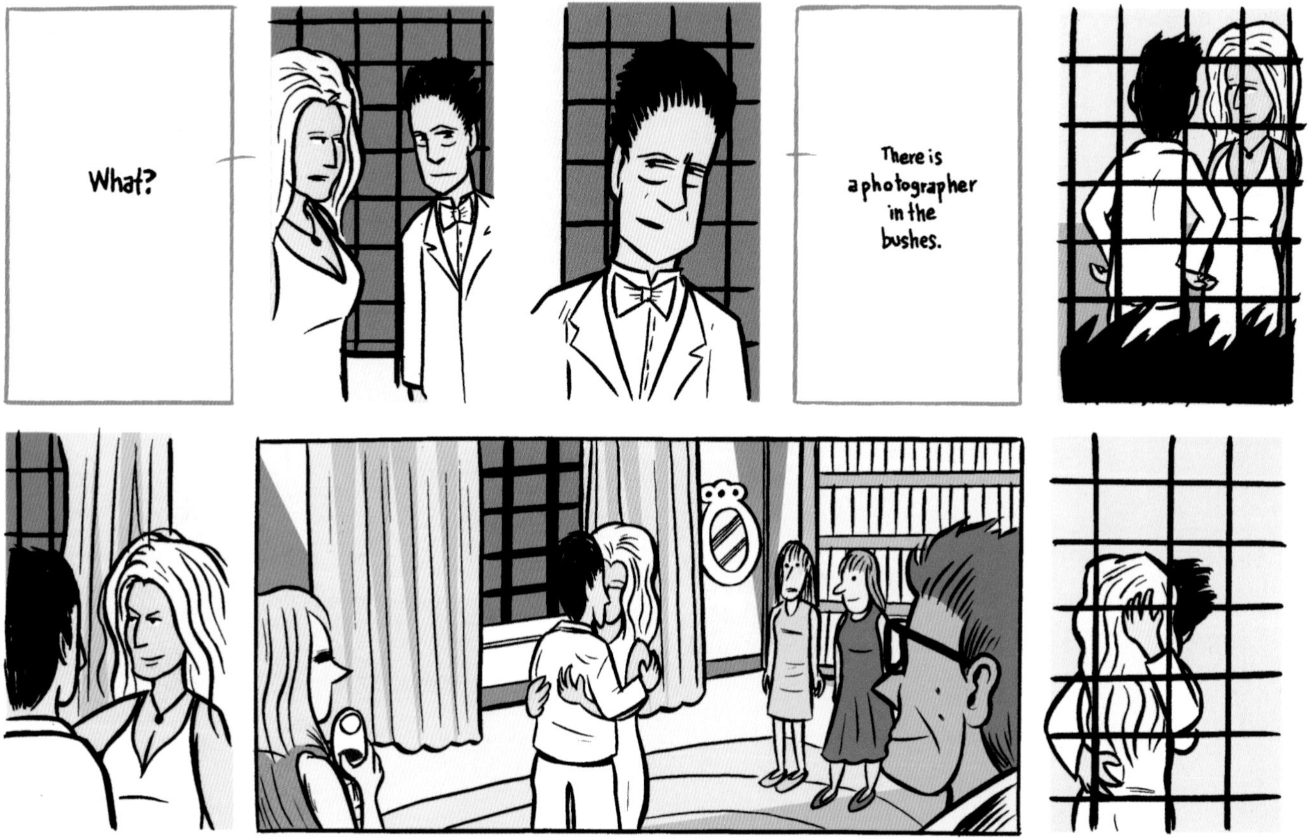
What?
There is a photographer in the bushes.

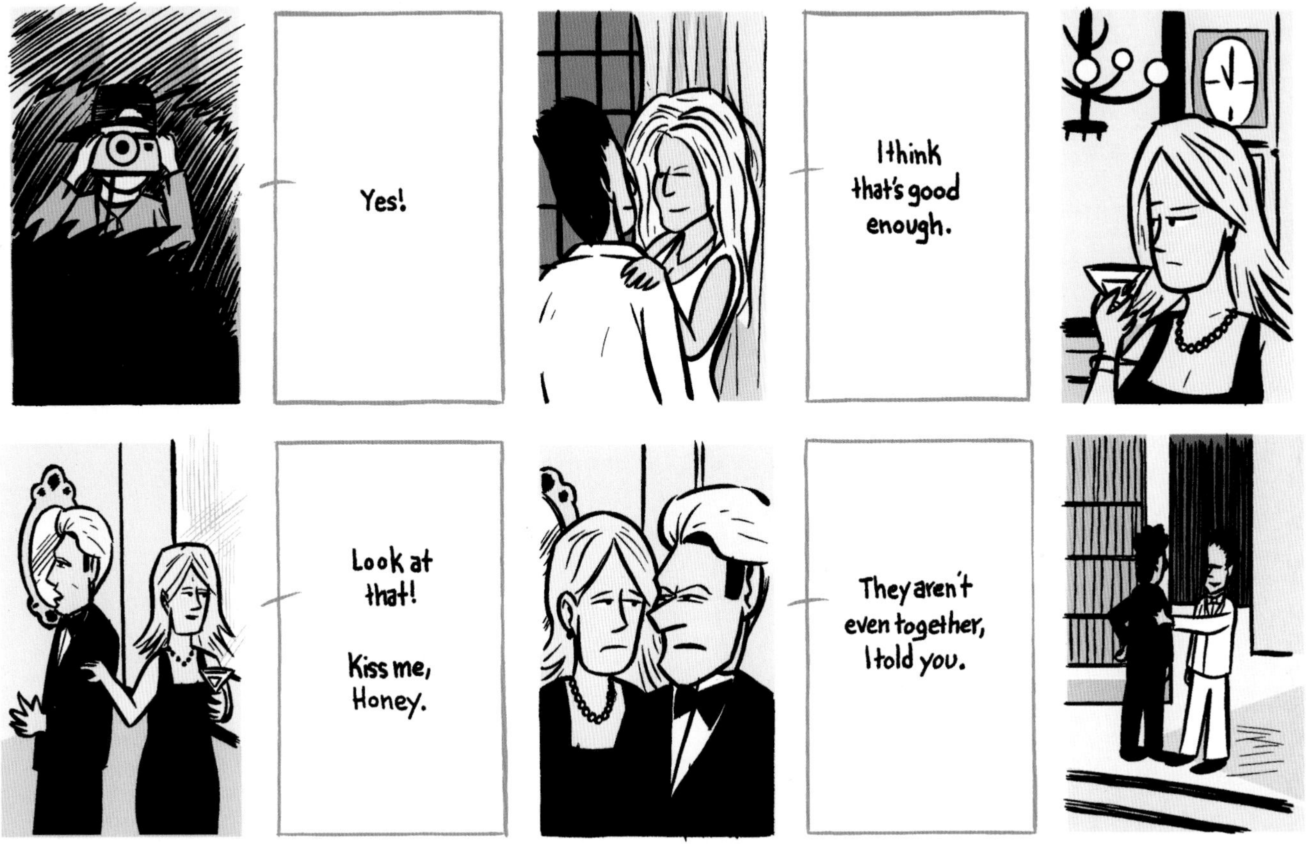
Yes!
I think that's good enough.
Look at that!
Kiss me, Honey.
They aren't even together, I told you.

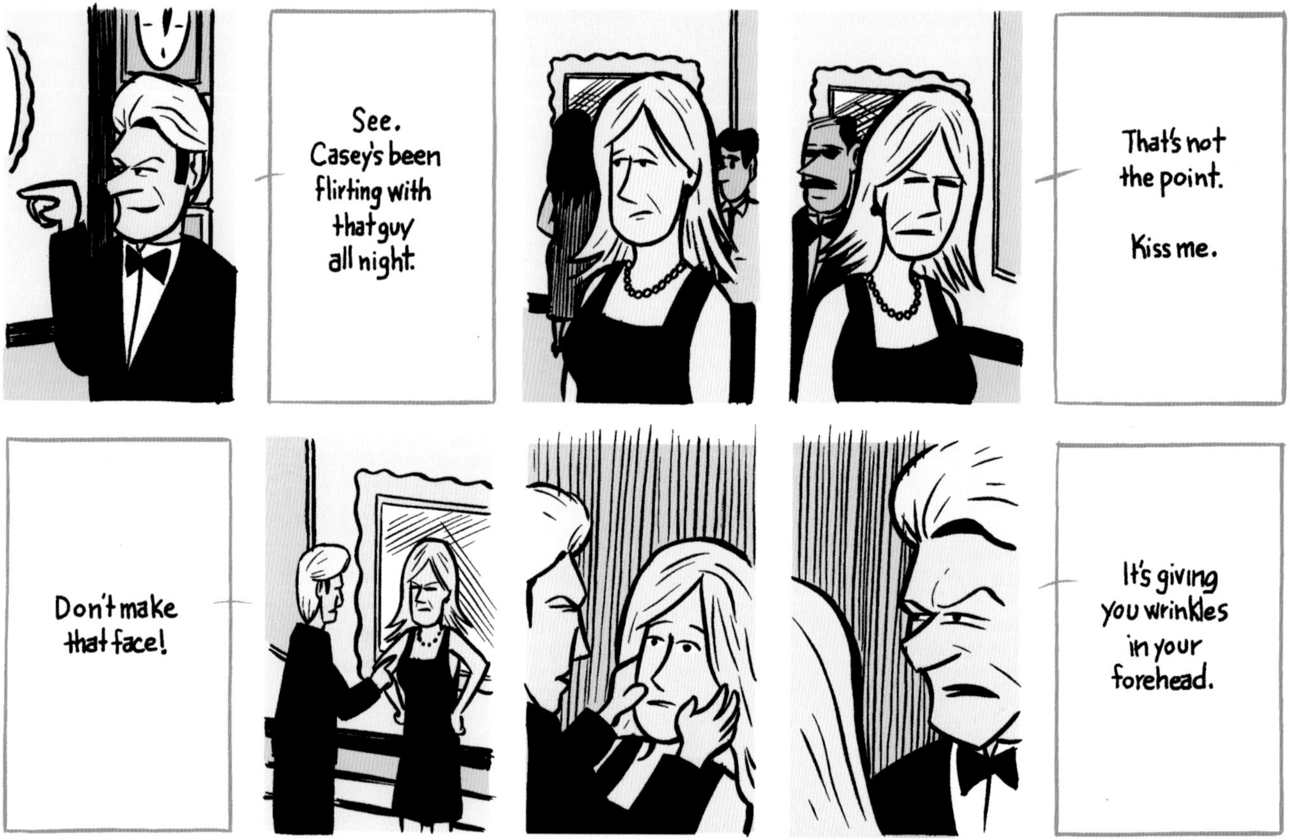
See.
Casey's been flirting with that guy all night.
That's not the point.
Kiss me.
Don't make that face!
It's giving you wrinkles in your forehead.

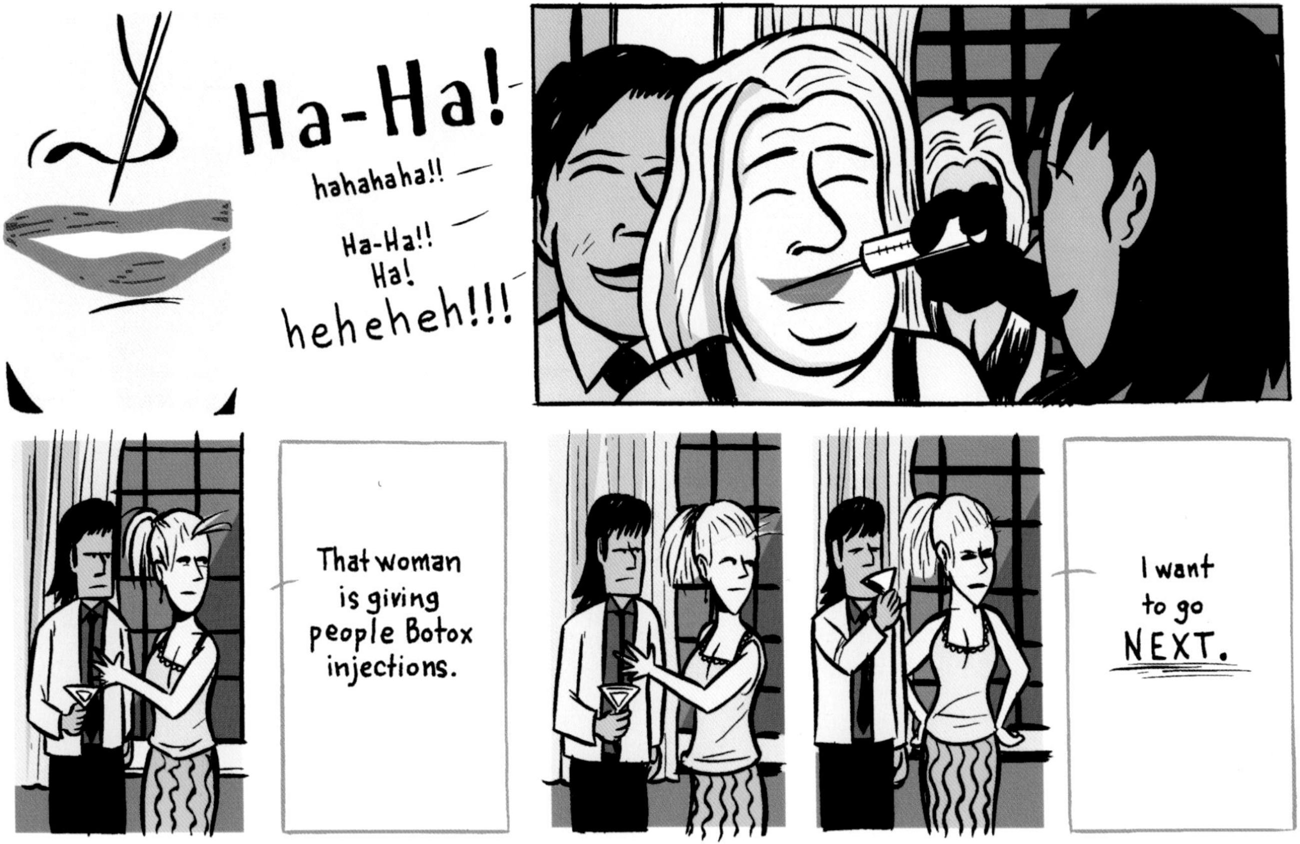
Ha-Ha!
hahahaha!!
Ha-Ha!! Ha!
heheheh!!!
That woman is giving people Botox injections.
I want to go NEXT.

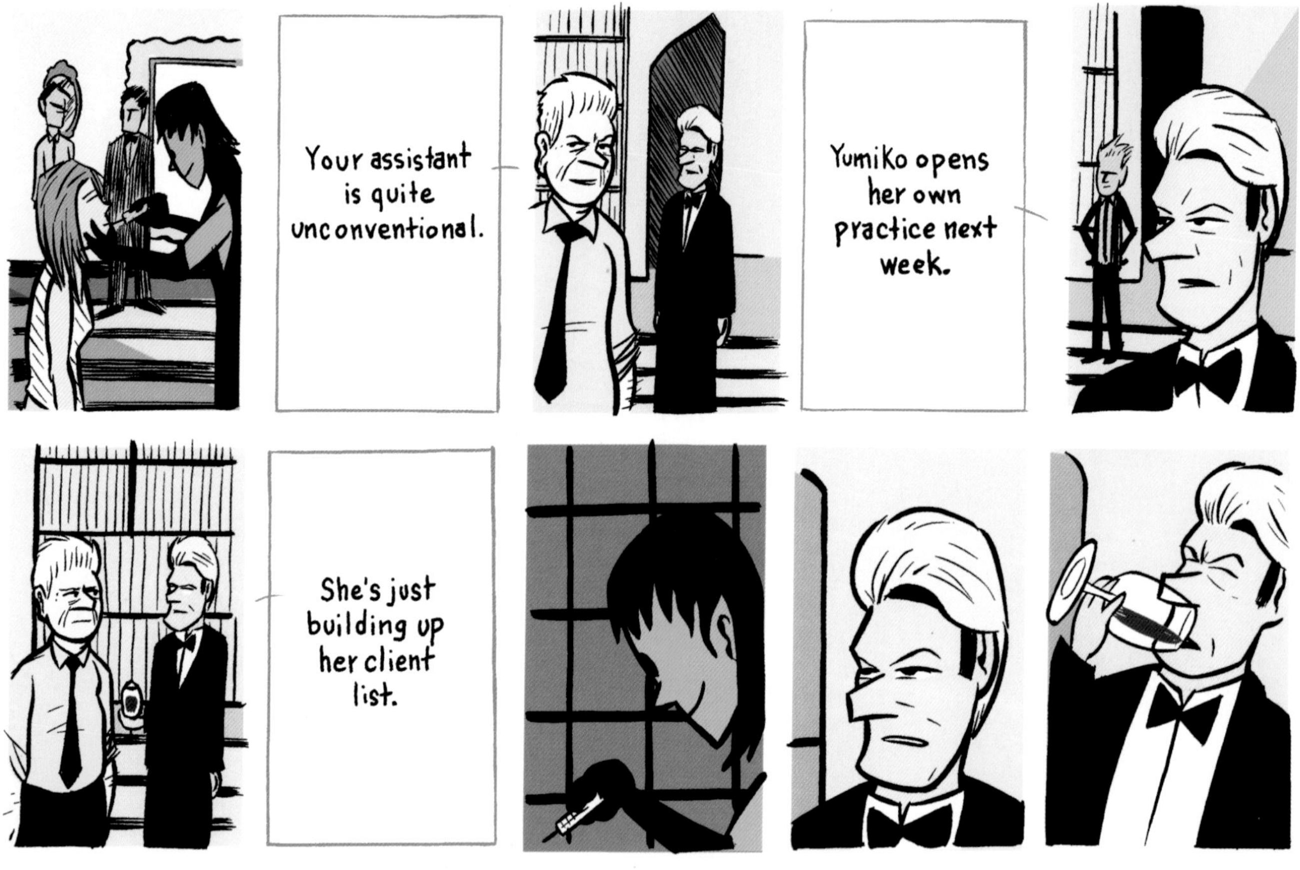
Your assistant is quite unconventional.
Yumiko opens her own practice next week.
She's just building up her client list.

34

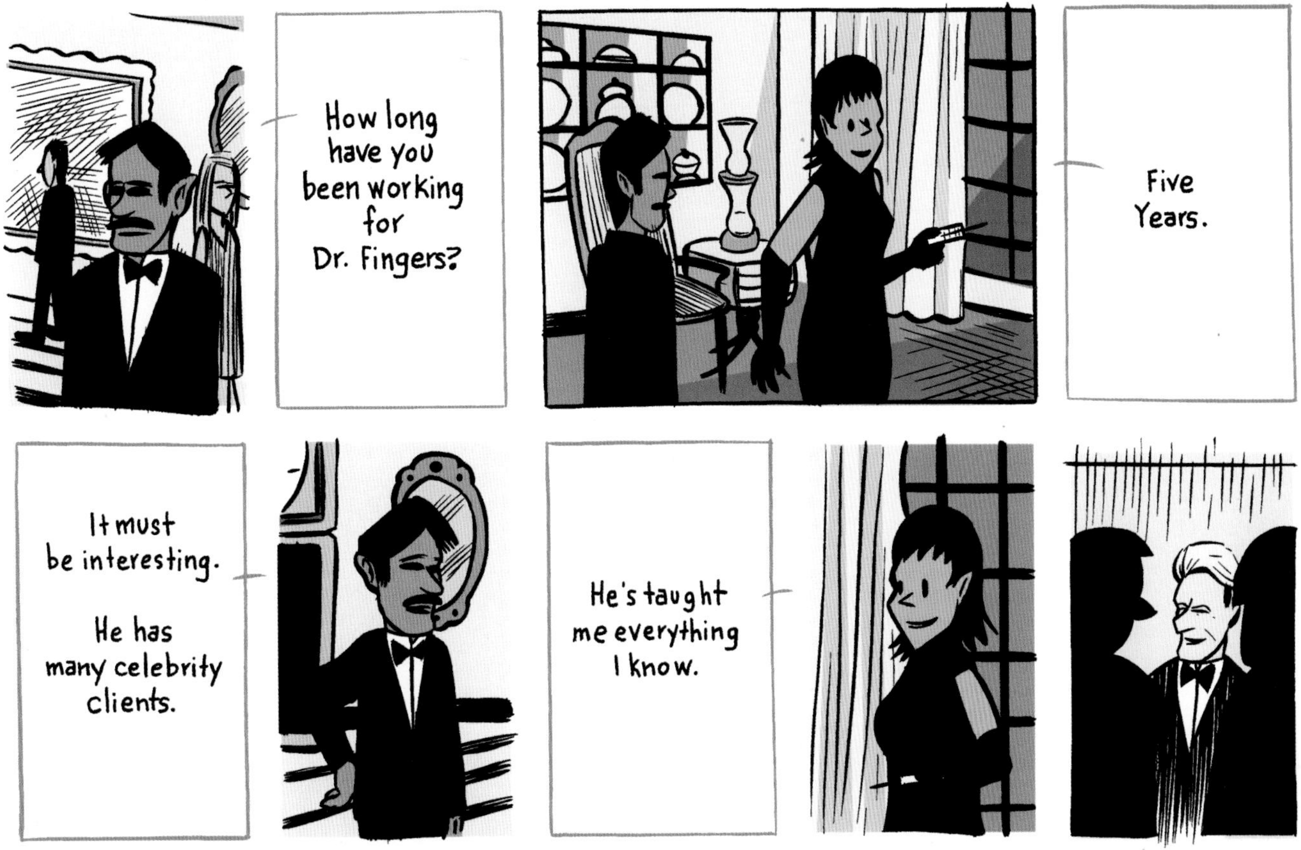
How long have you been working for Dr. Fingers?
Five Years.
It must be interesting.
He has many celebrity clients.
He's taught me everything I know.

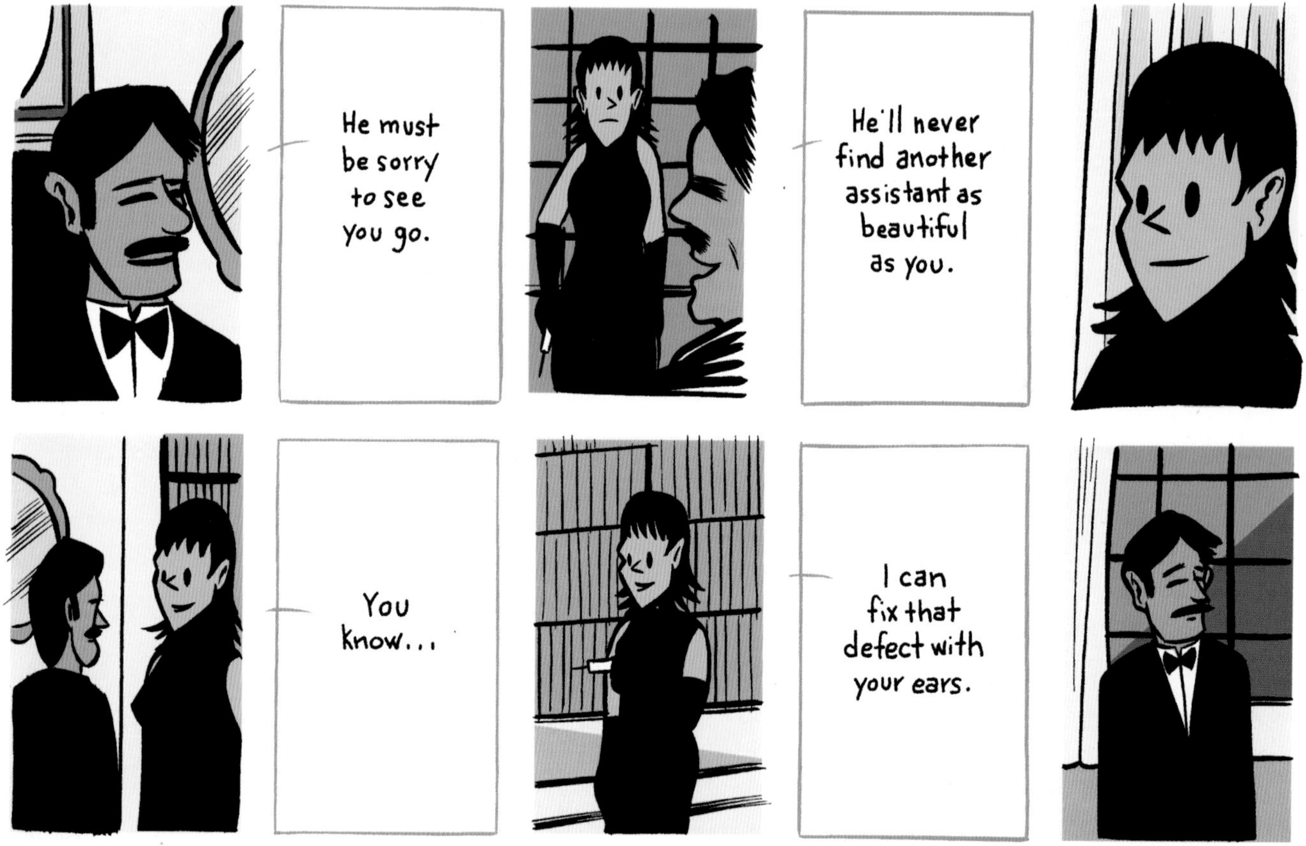
He must be sorry to see you go.
He'll never find another assistant as beautiful as you.
You know...
I can fix that defect with your ears.

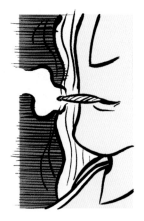

OH!

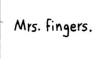

Mrs. Fingers.

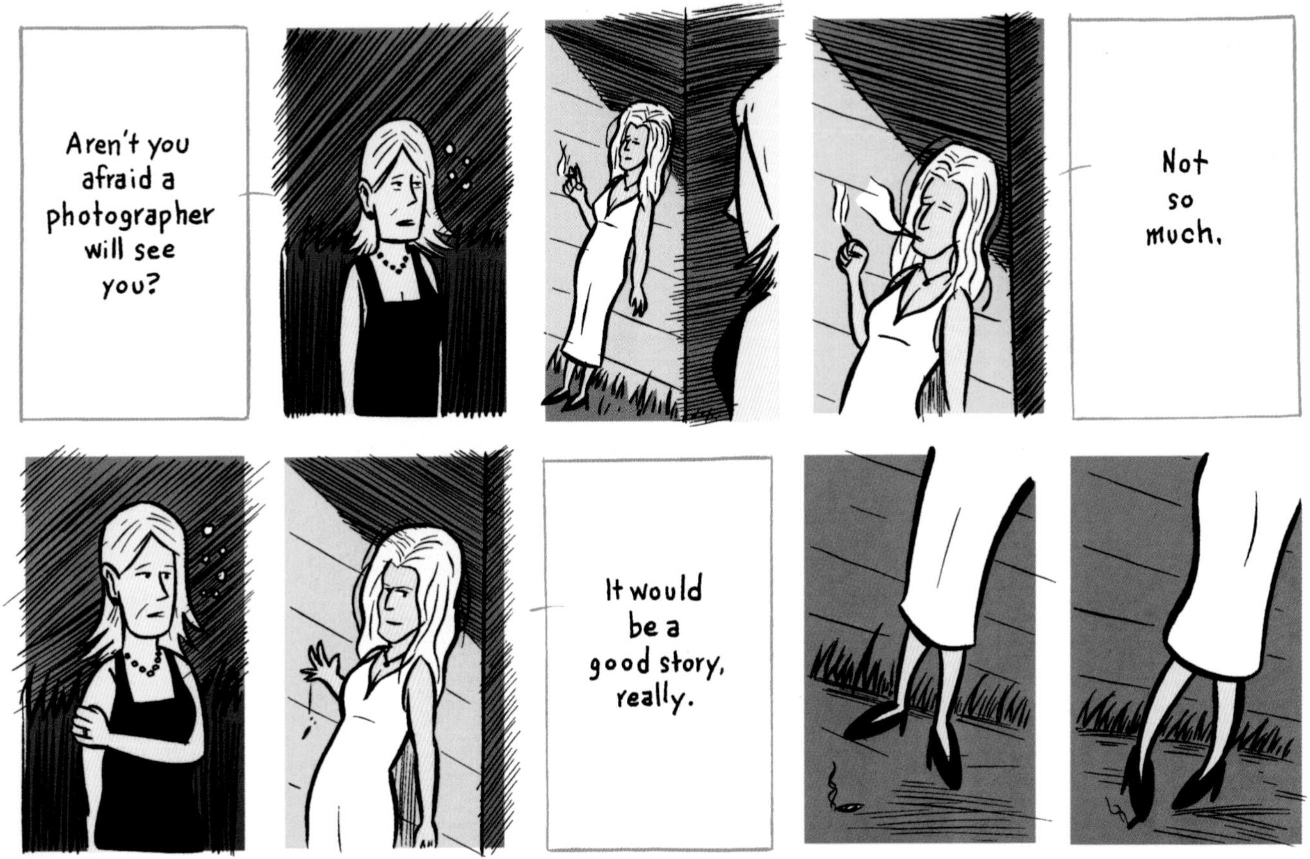
Aren't you afraid a photographer will see you?
Not so much.
It would be a good story, really.

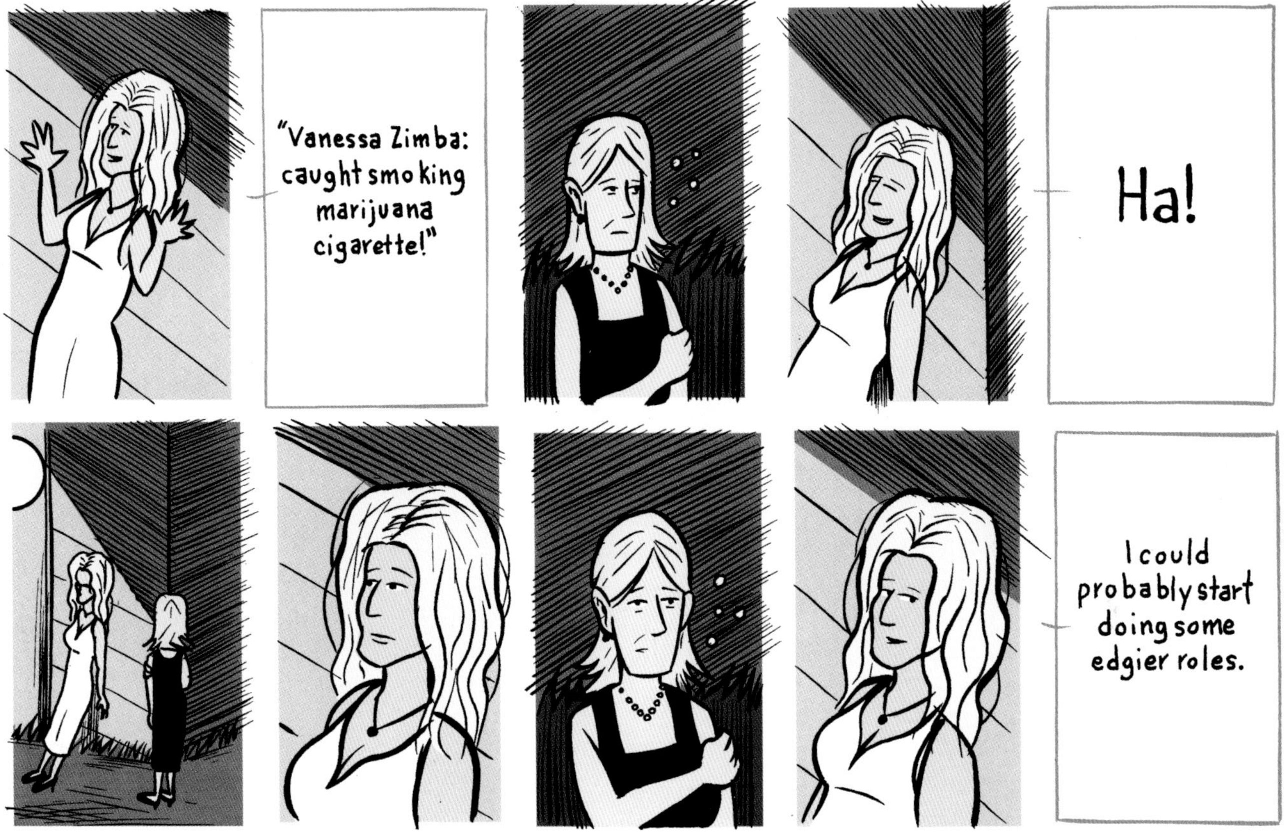
"Vanessa Zimba: caught smoking marijuana cigarette!"
Ha!
I could probably start doing some edgier roles.

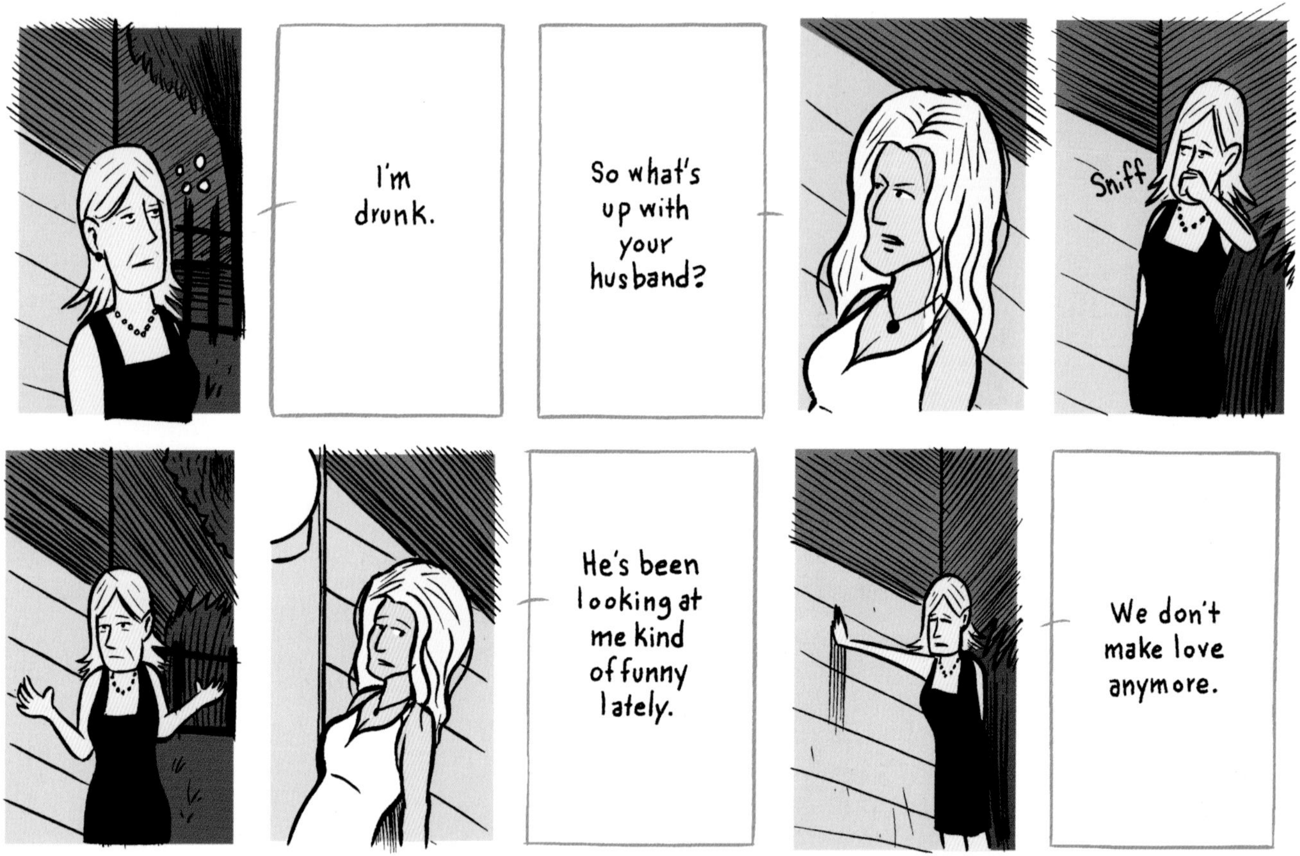
I'm drunk.
So what's up with your husband?
Sniff
He's been looking at me kind of funny lately.
We don't make love anymore.

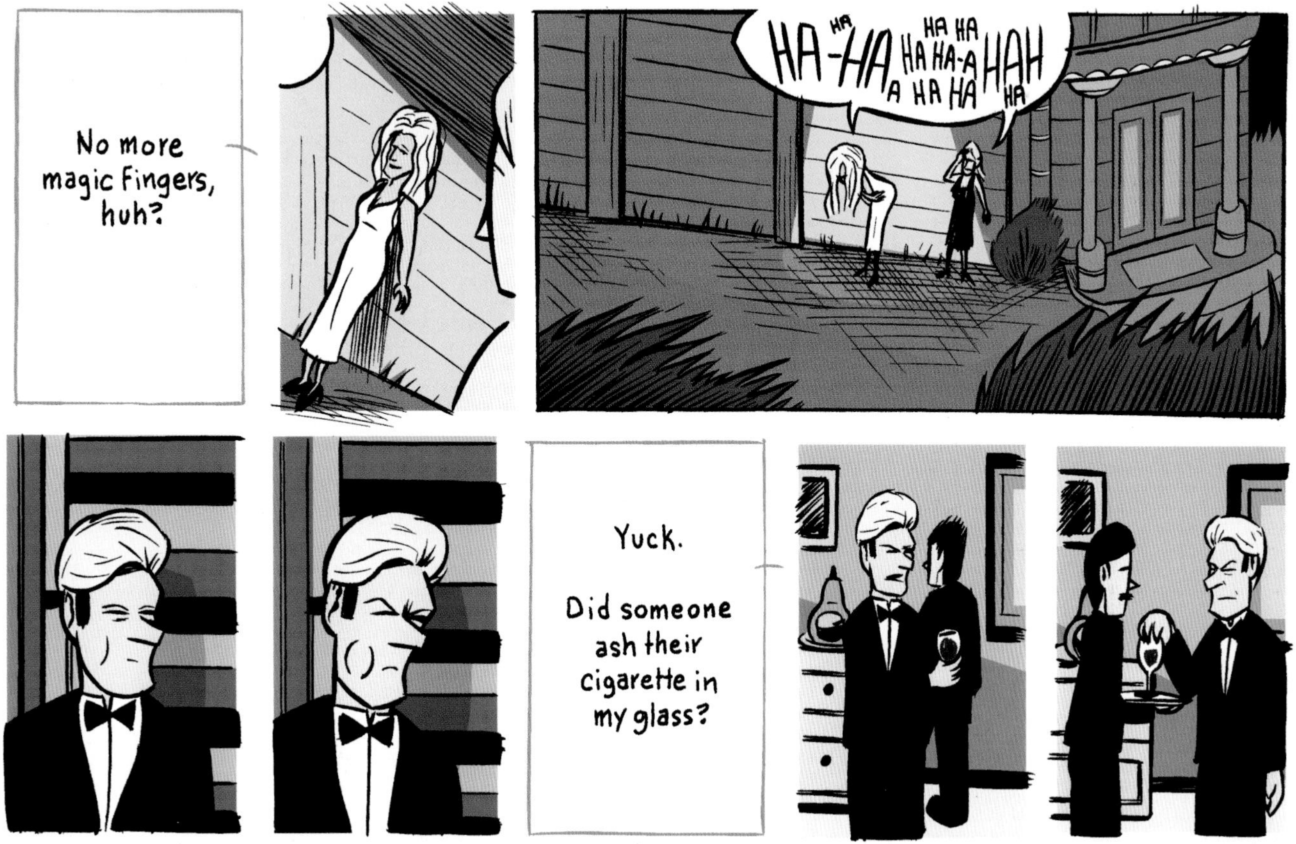
No more magic fingers, huh?
HA-HA HA HA HA HA HA HA-A A HA HA HAH HA
Yuck.
Did someone ash their cigarette in my glass?

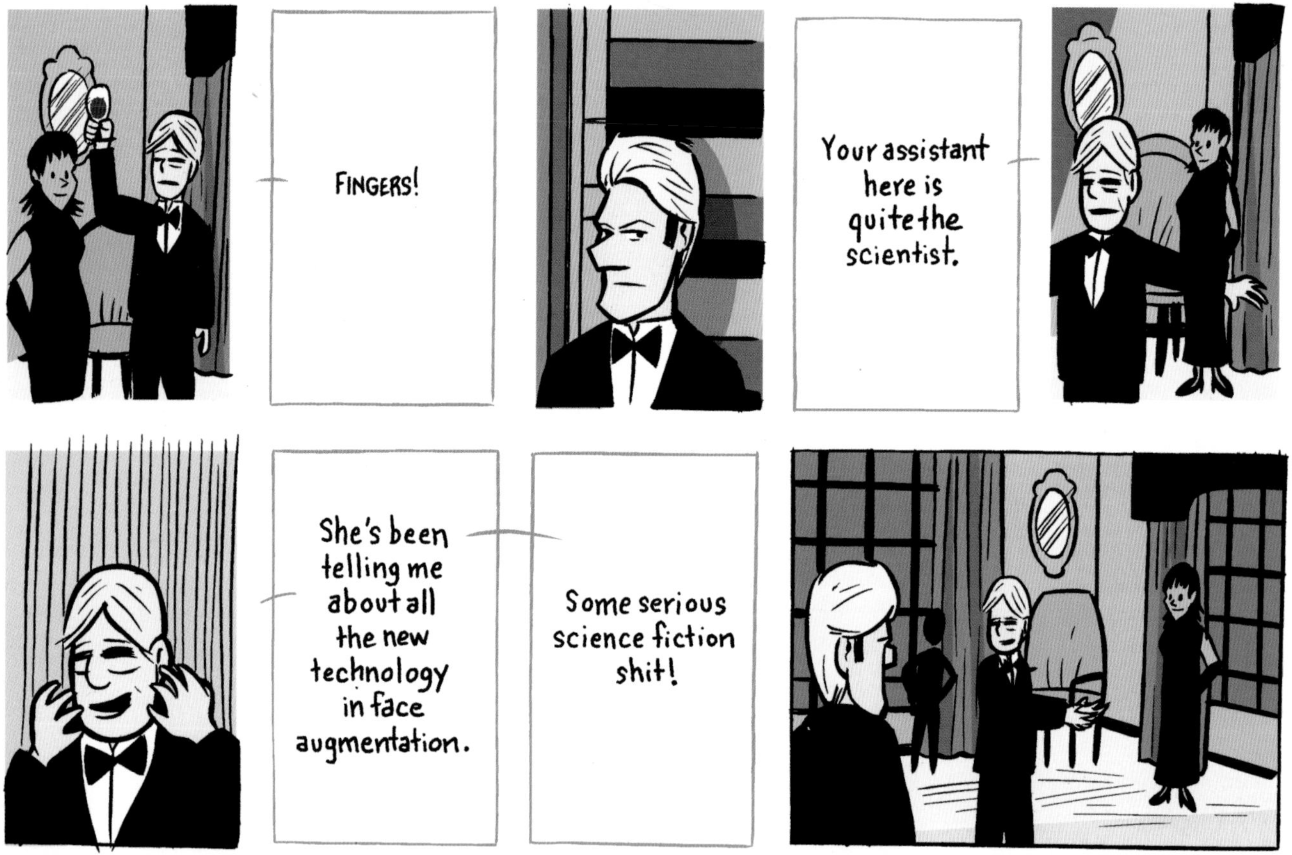
FINGERS!
Your assistant here is quite the scientist.
She's been telling me about all the new technology in face augmentation.
Some serious science fiction shit!

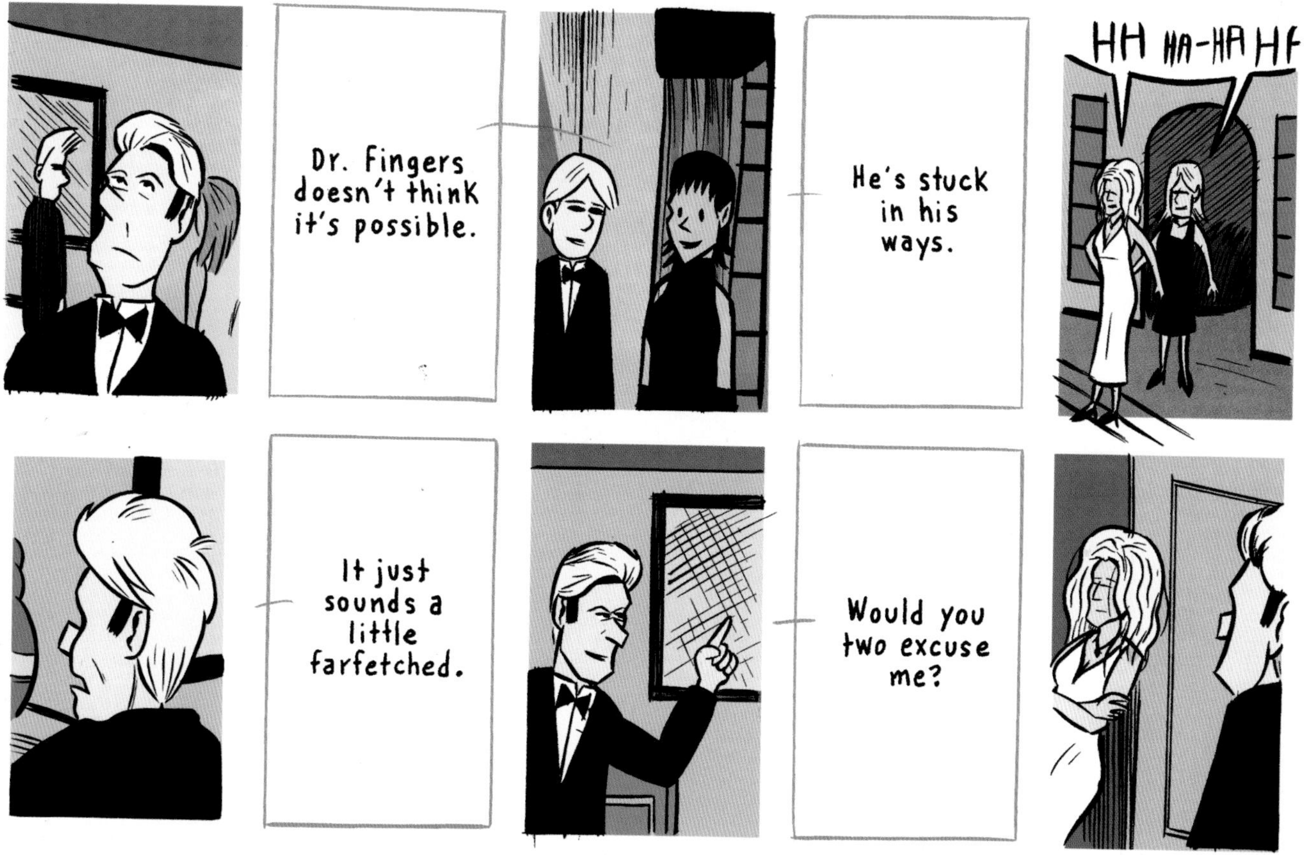
Dr. Fingers doesn't think it's possible.
He's stuck in his ways.
HH HA-HA HF
It just sounds a little farfetched.
Would you two excuse me?

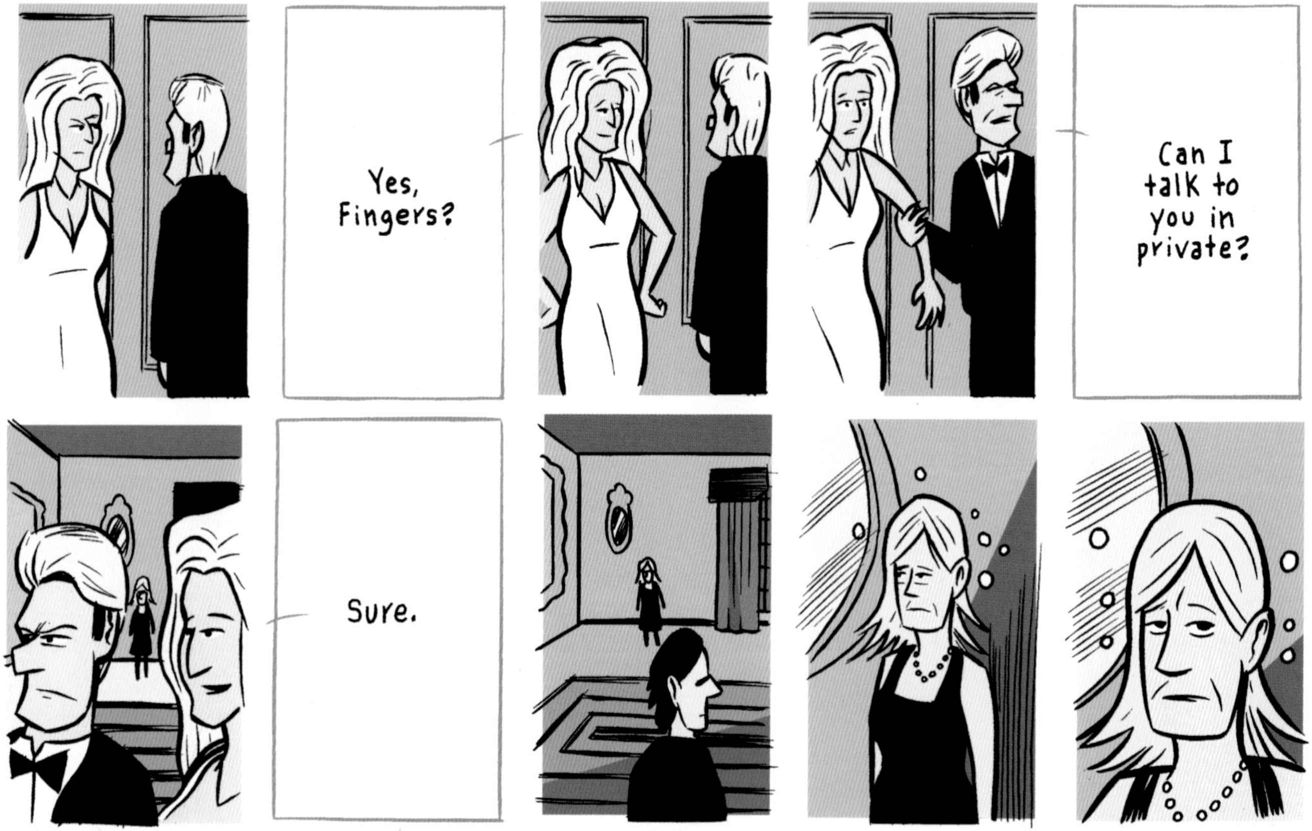
Yes, Fingers?
Can I talk to you in private?
Sure.

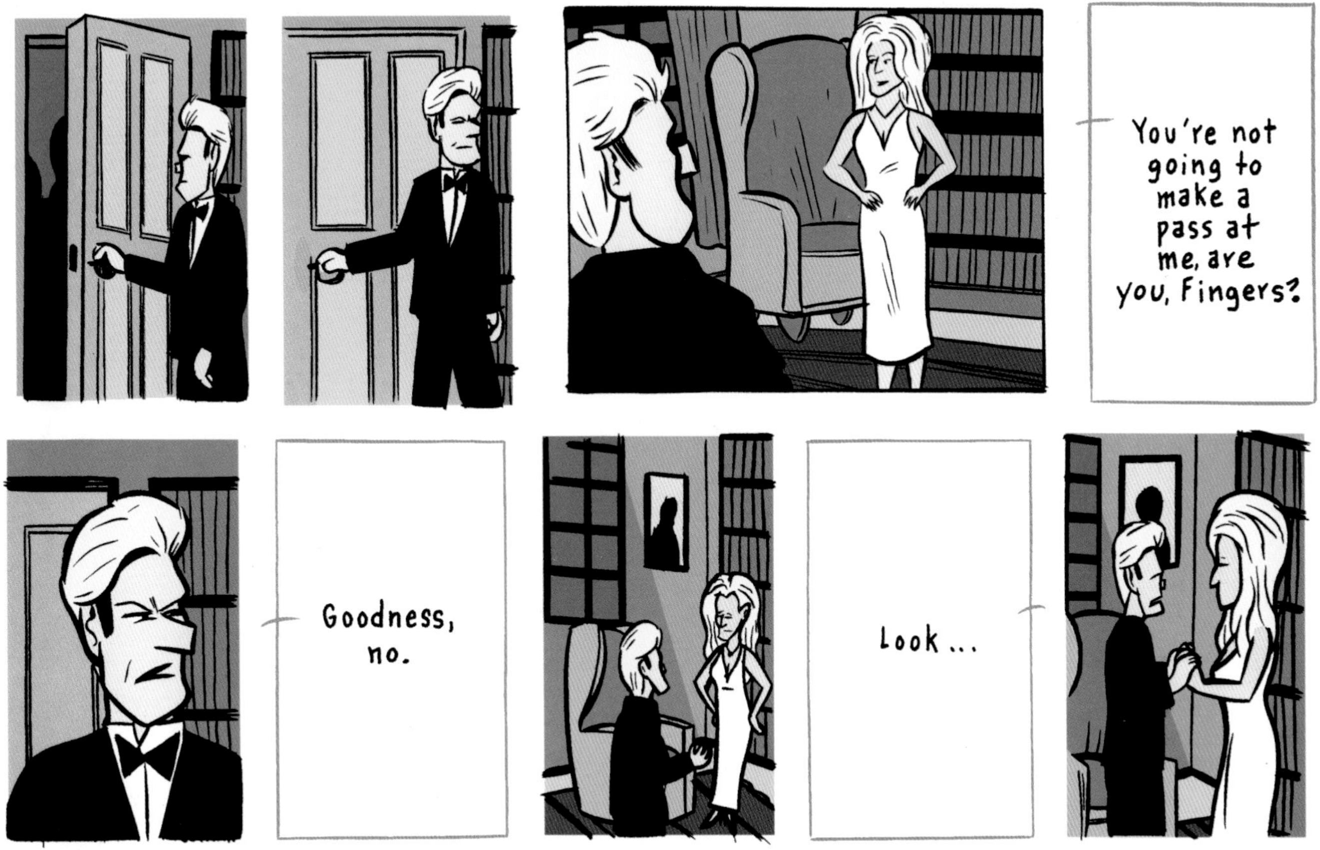
You're not going to make a pass at me, are you, Fingers?
Goodness, no.
Look ...

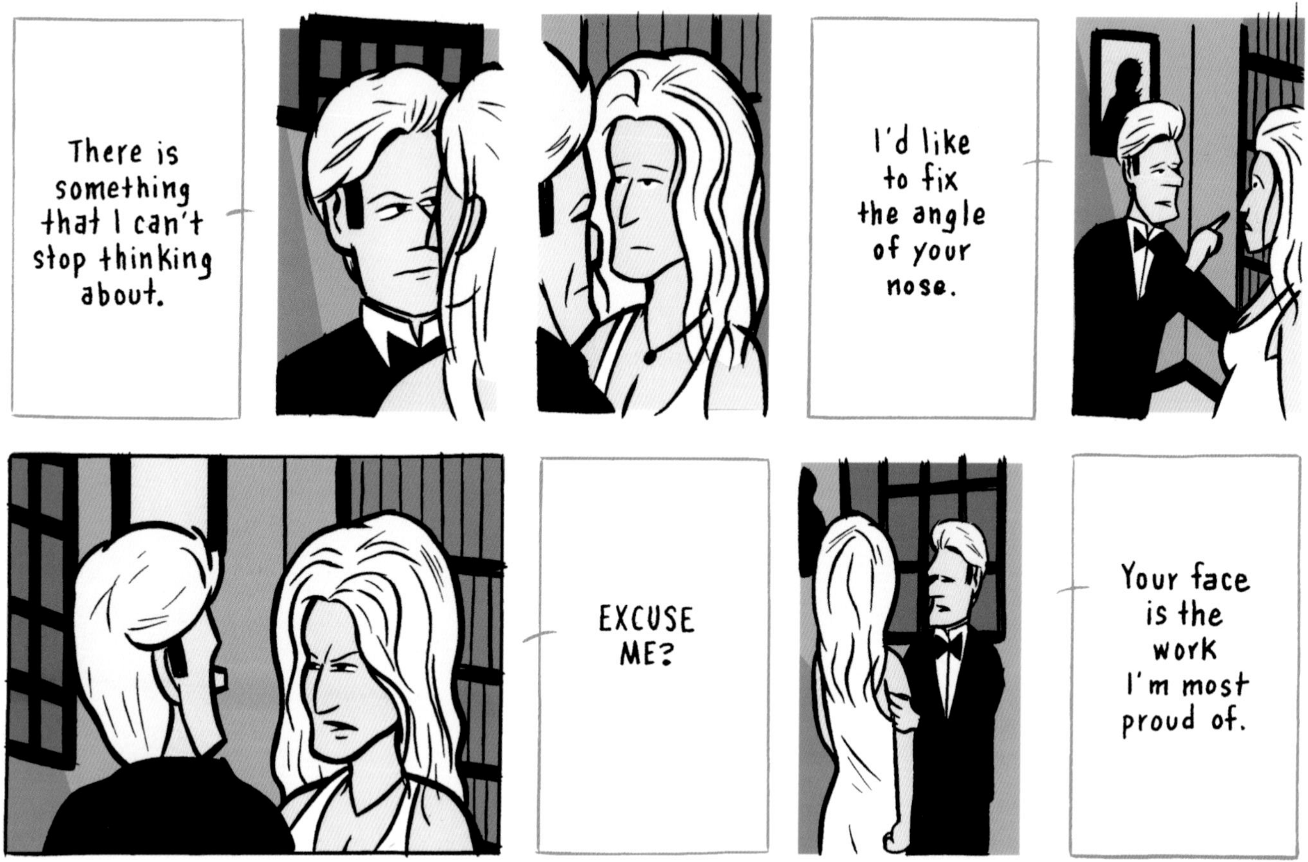
There is something that I can't stop thinking about.
I'd like to fix the angle of your nose.
EXCUSE ME?
Your face is the work I'm most proud of.

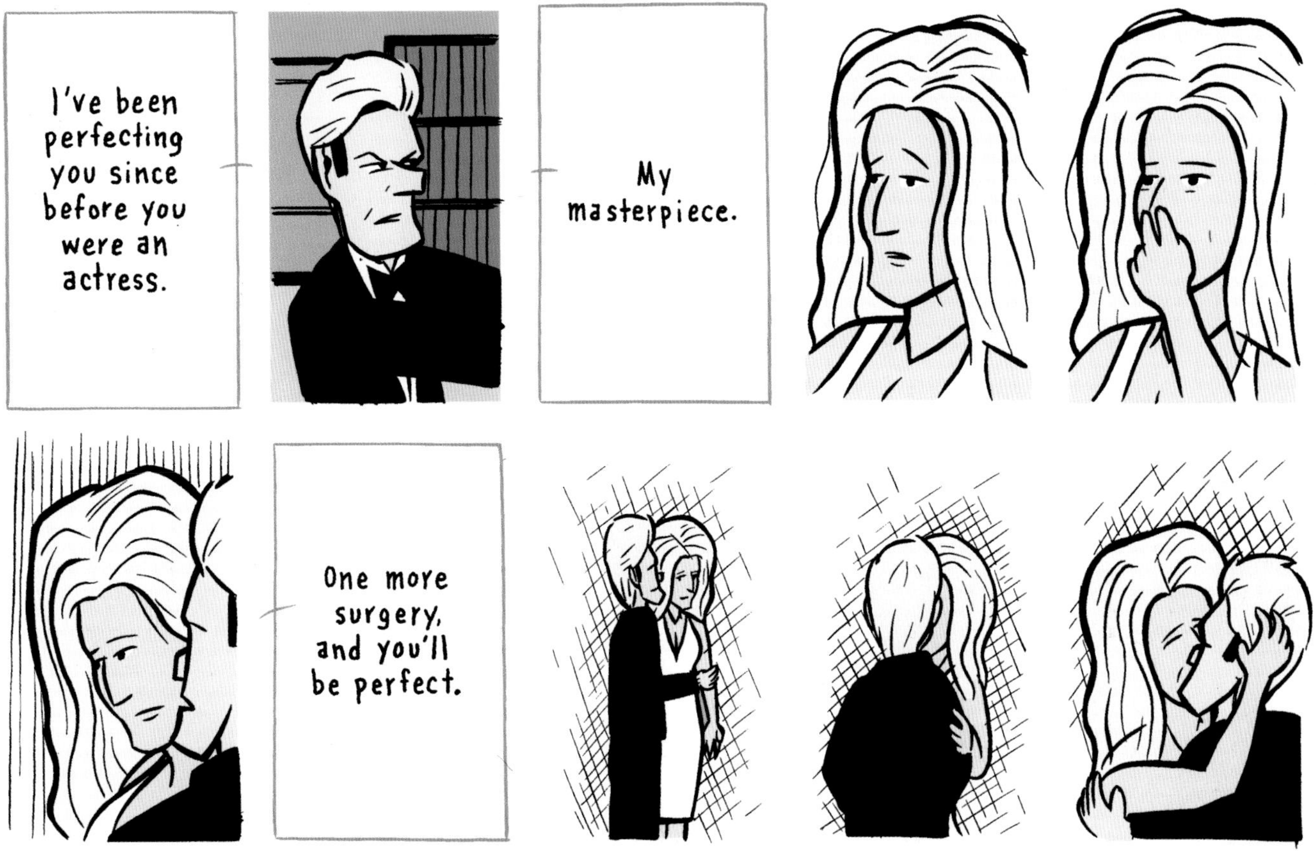
I've been perfecting you since before you were an actress.
My masterpiece.
One more surgery, and you'll be perfect.

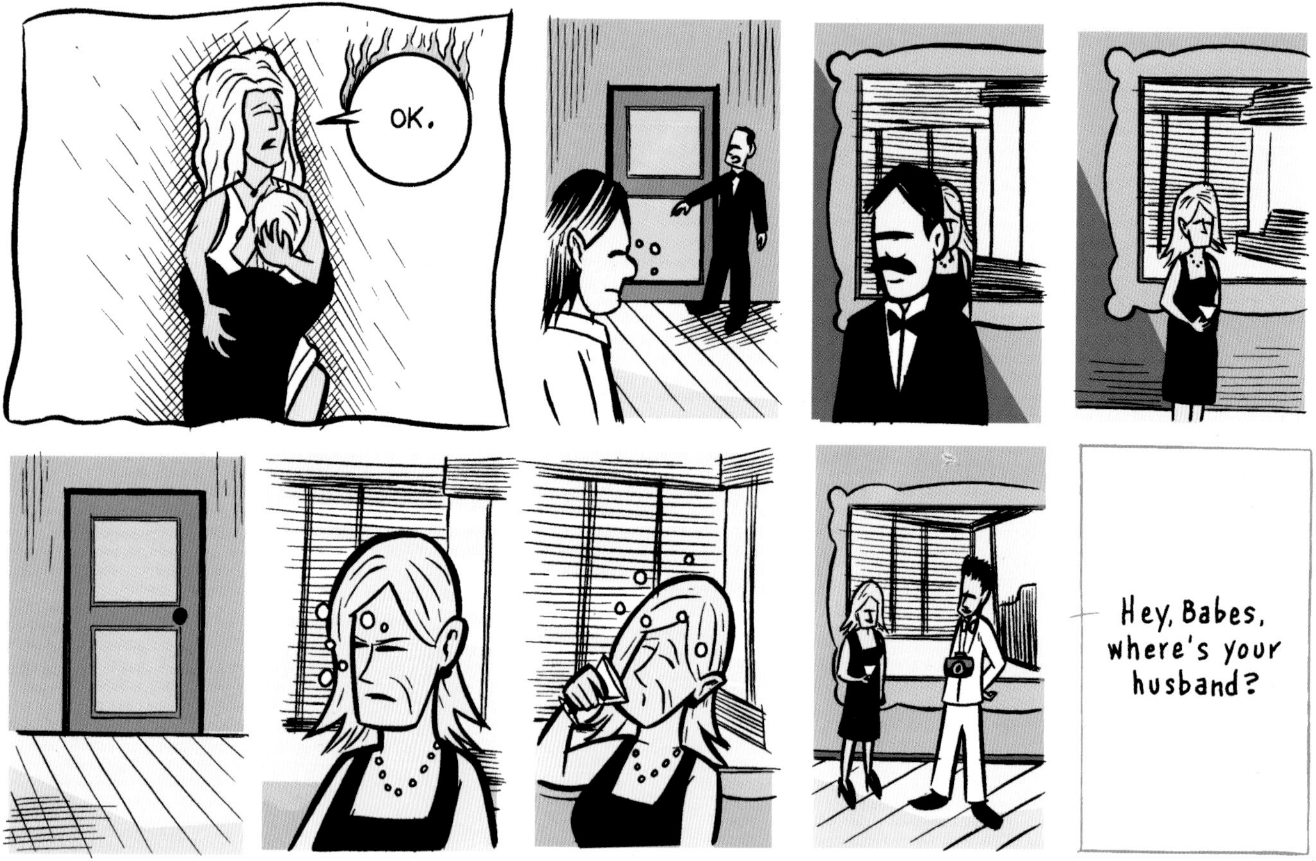
OK.
Hey, Babes, where's your husband?

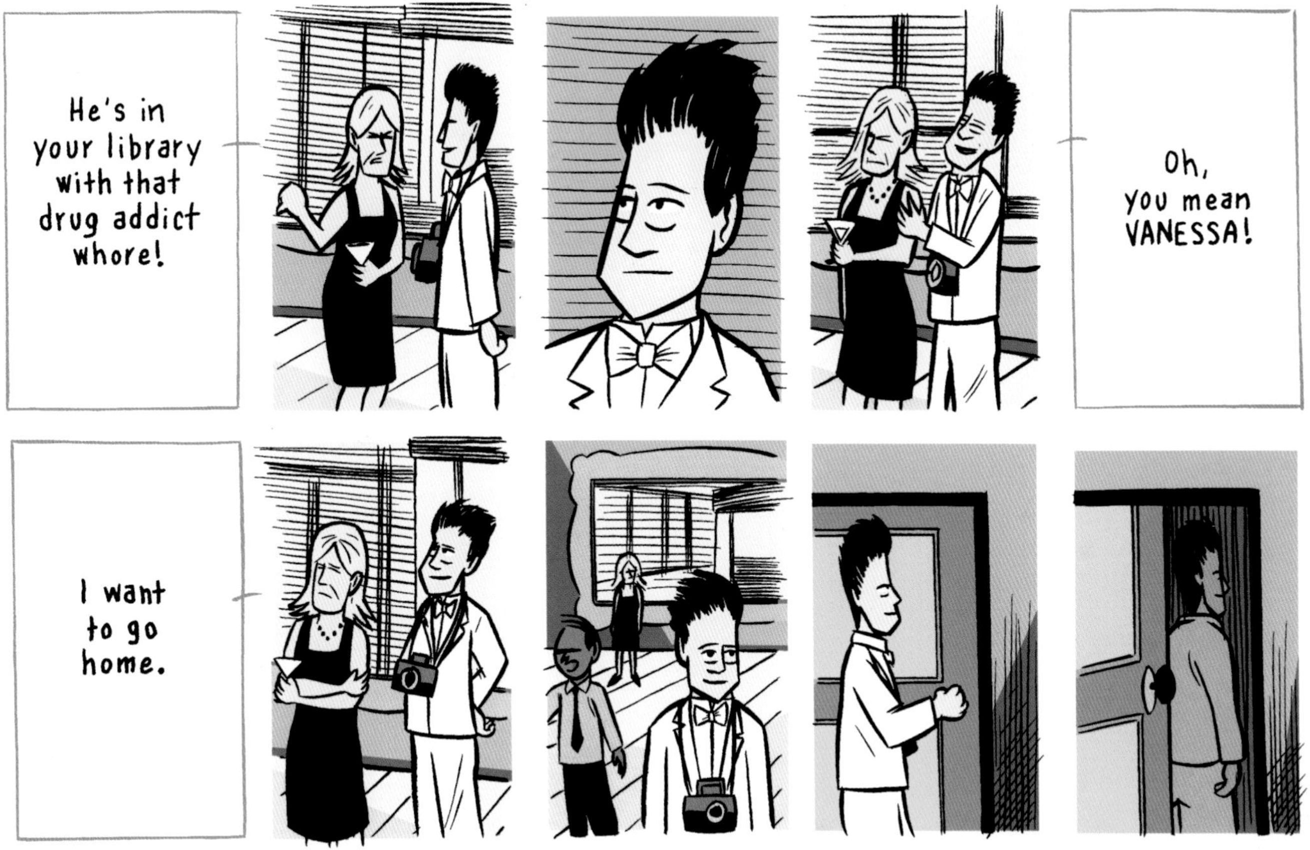
He's in your library with that drug addict whore!
Oh, you mean VANESSA!
I want to go home.

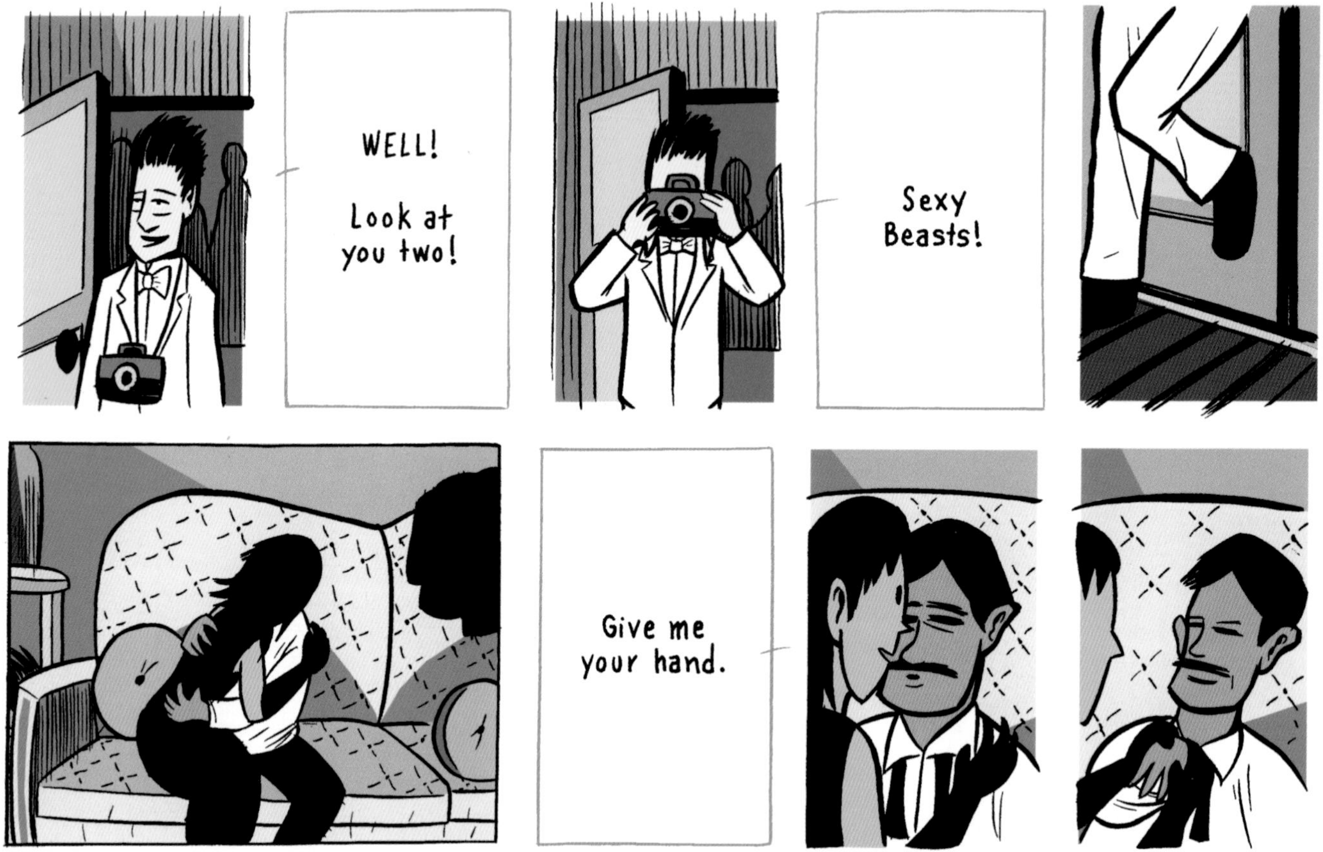
WELL!
Look at you two!
Sexy Beasts!
Give me your hand.

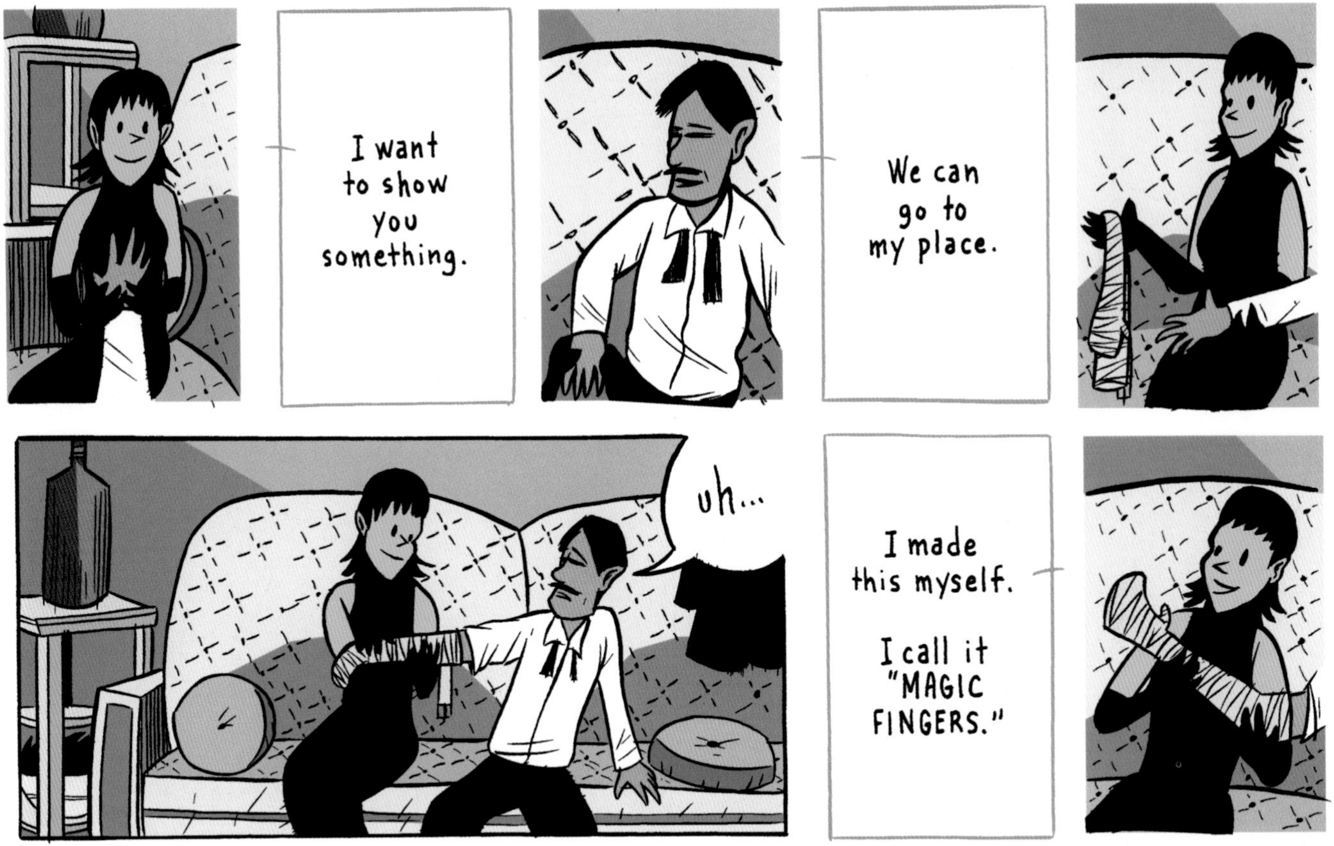
I want to show you something.
We can go to my place.
uh...
I made this myself.
I call it "MAGIC FINGERS."

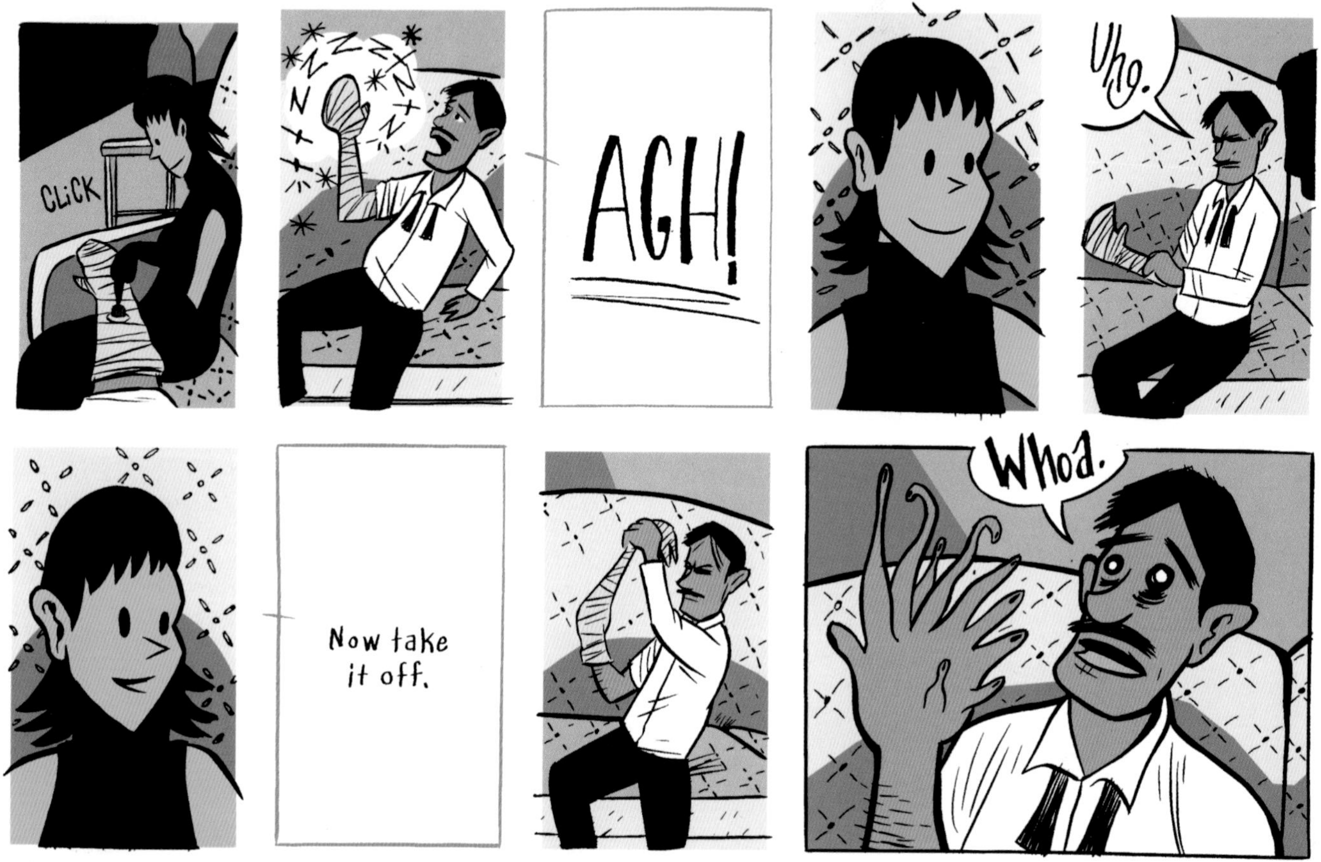
CLICK
AGH!
Uhg.
Now take it off.
Whoa.

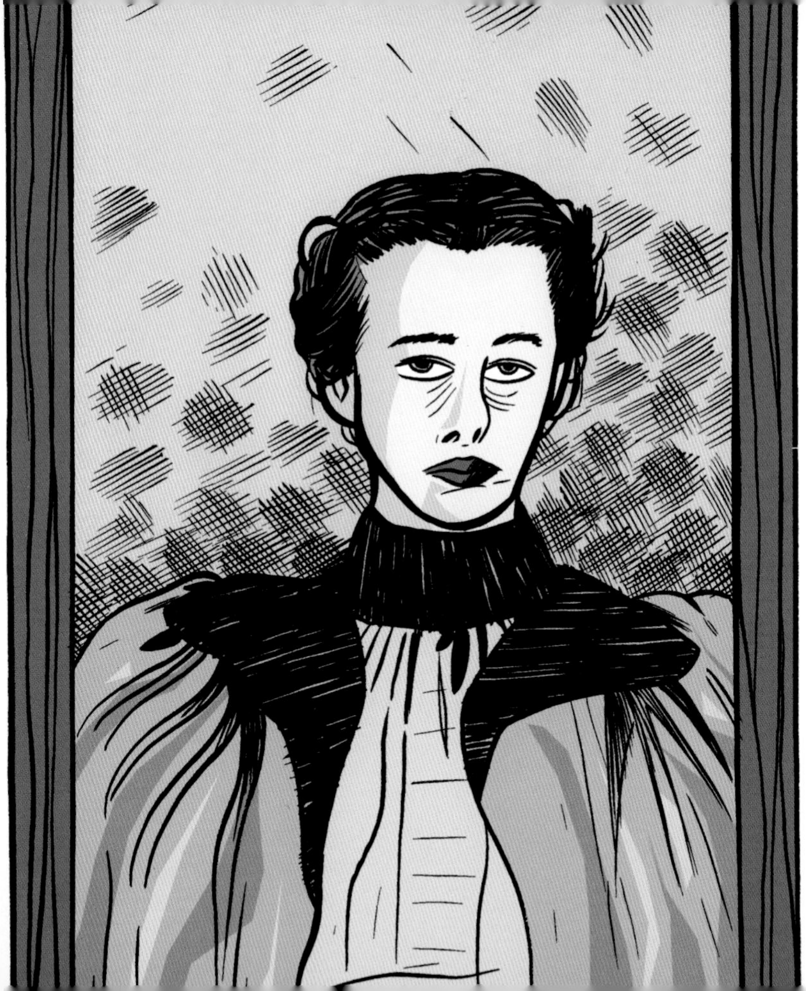

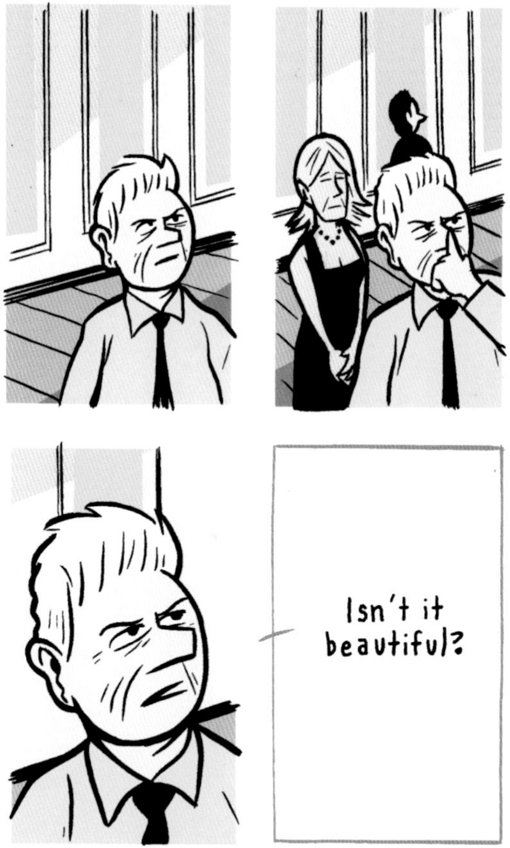
Isn't it beautiful?

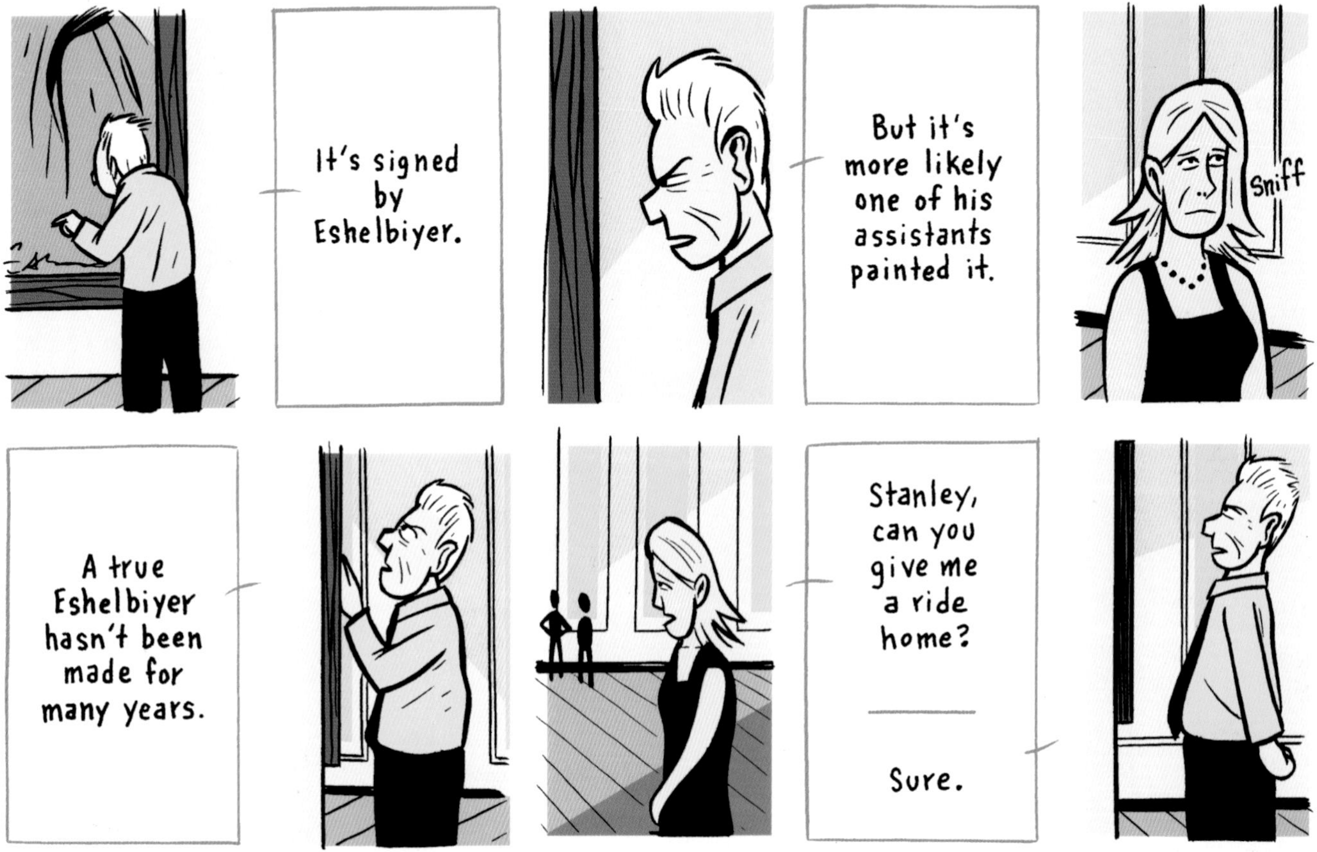
It's signed by Eshelbiyer.
But it's more likely one of his assistants painted it.
Sniff
A true Eshelbiyer hasn't been made for many years.
Stanley, can you give me a ride home?
Sure.

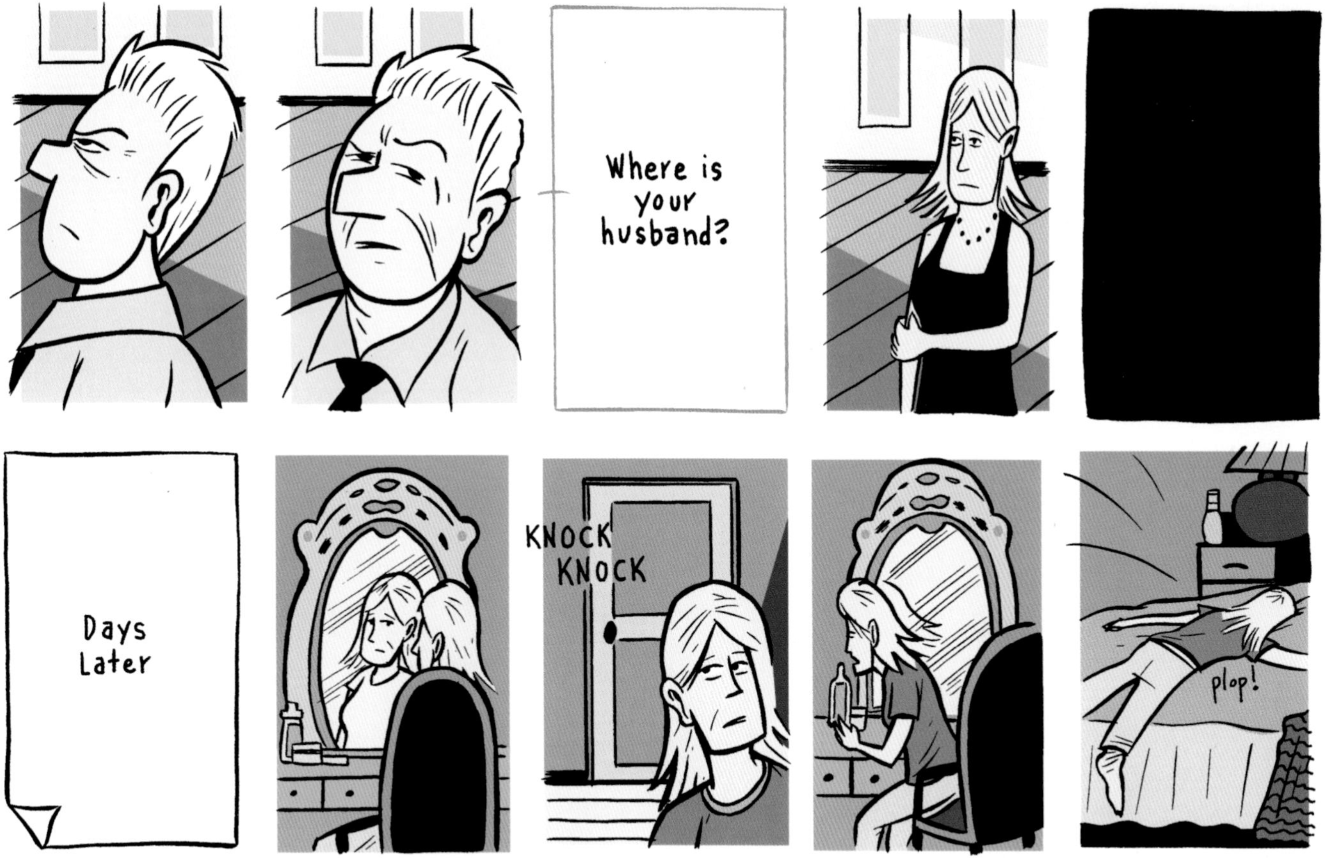
Where is your husband?
Days Later
KNOCK KNOCK
plop!

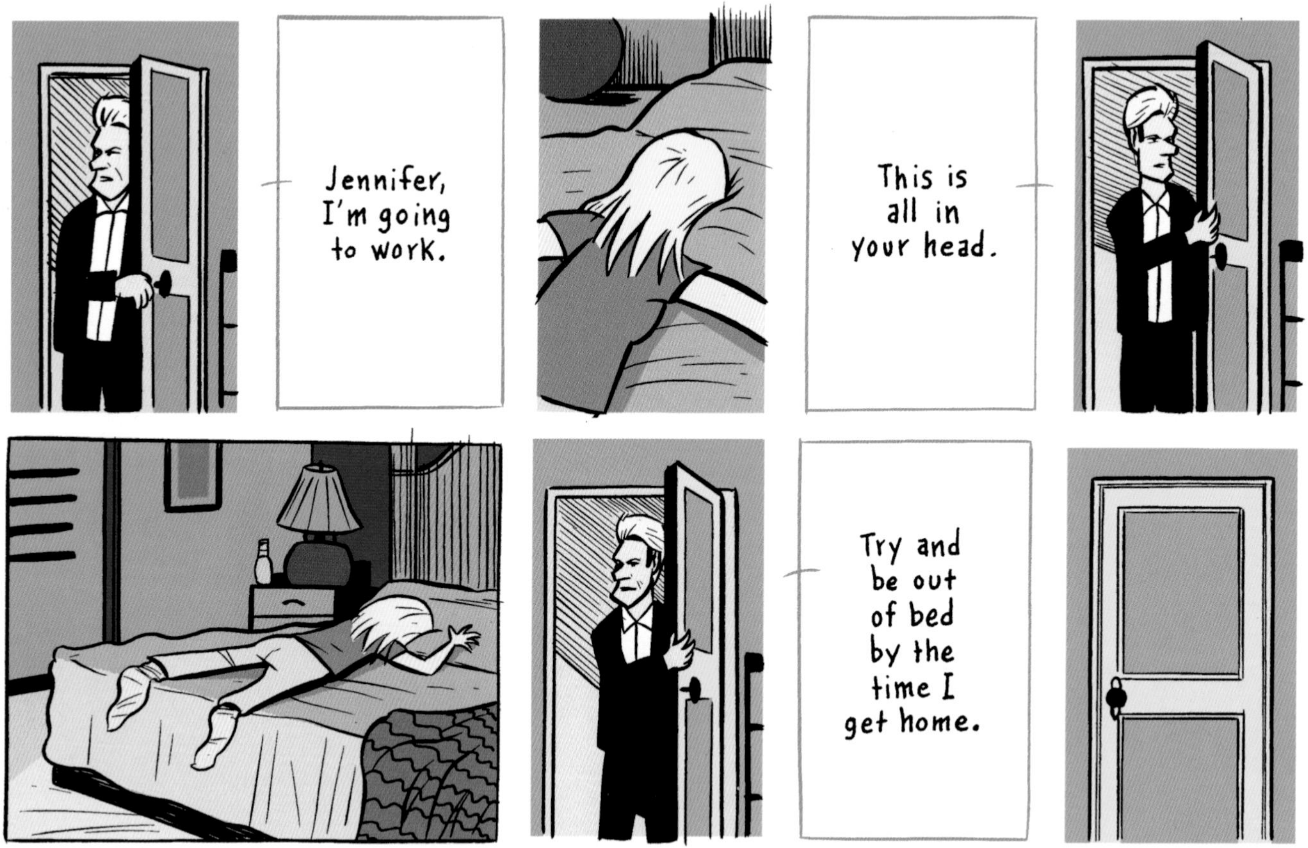
Jennifer,
I'm going
to work.
This is
all in
your head.
Try and
be out
of bed
by the
time I
get home.

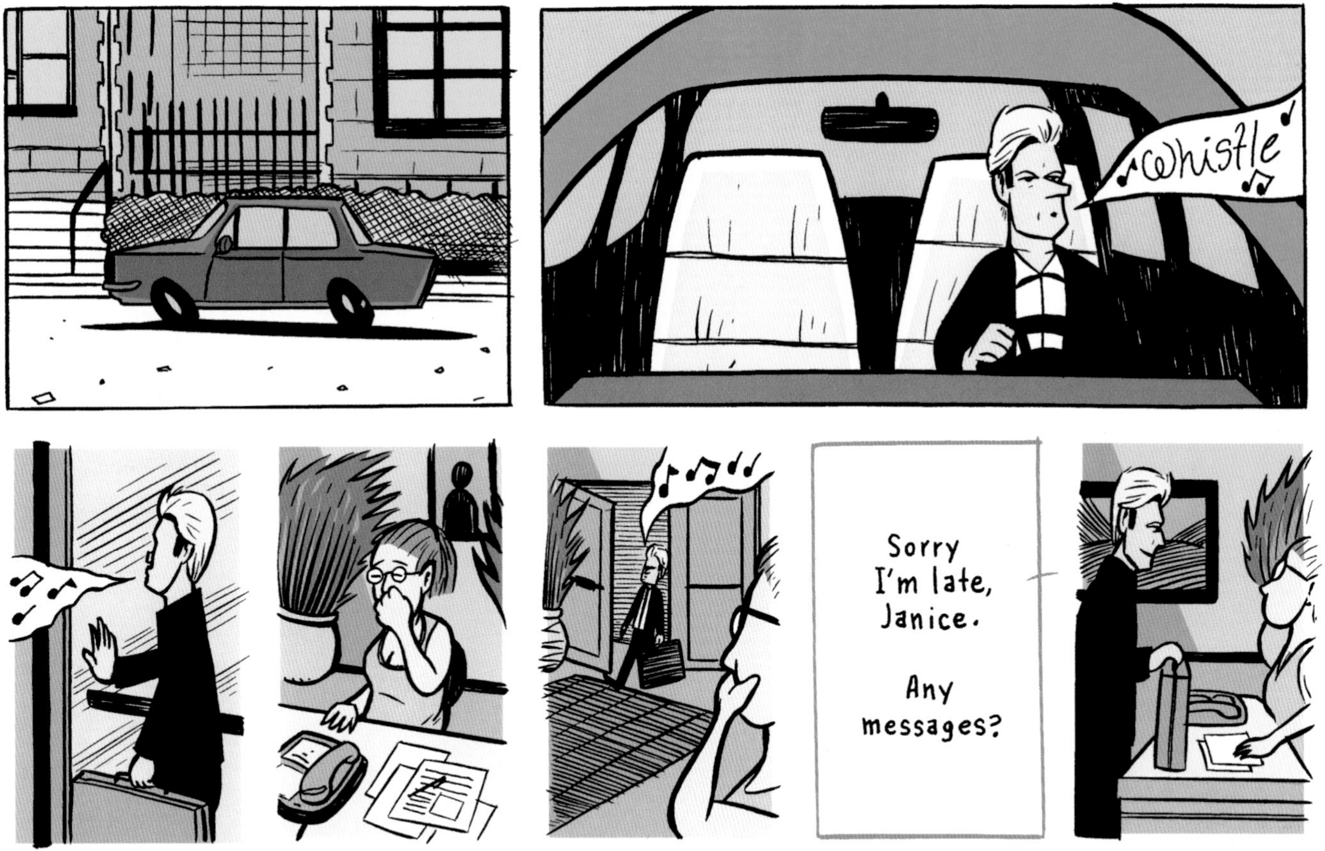
Whistle
Sorry I'm late, Janice.
Any messages?

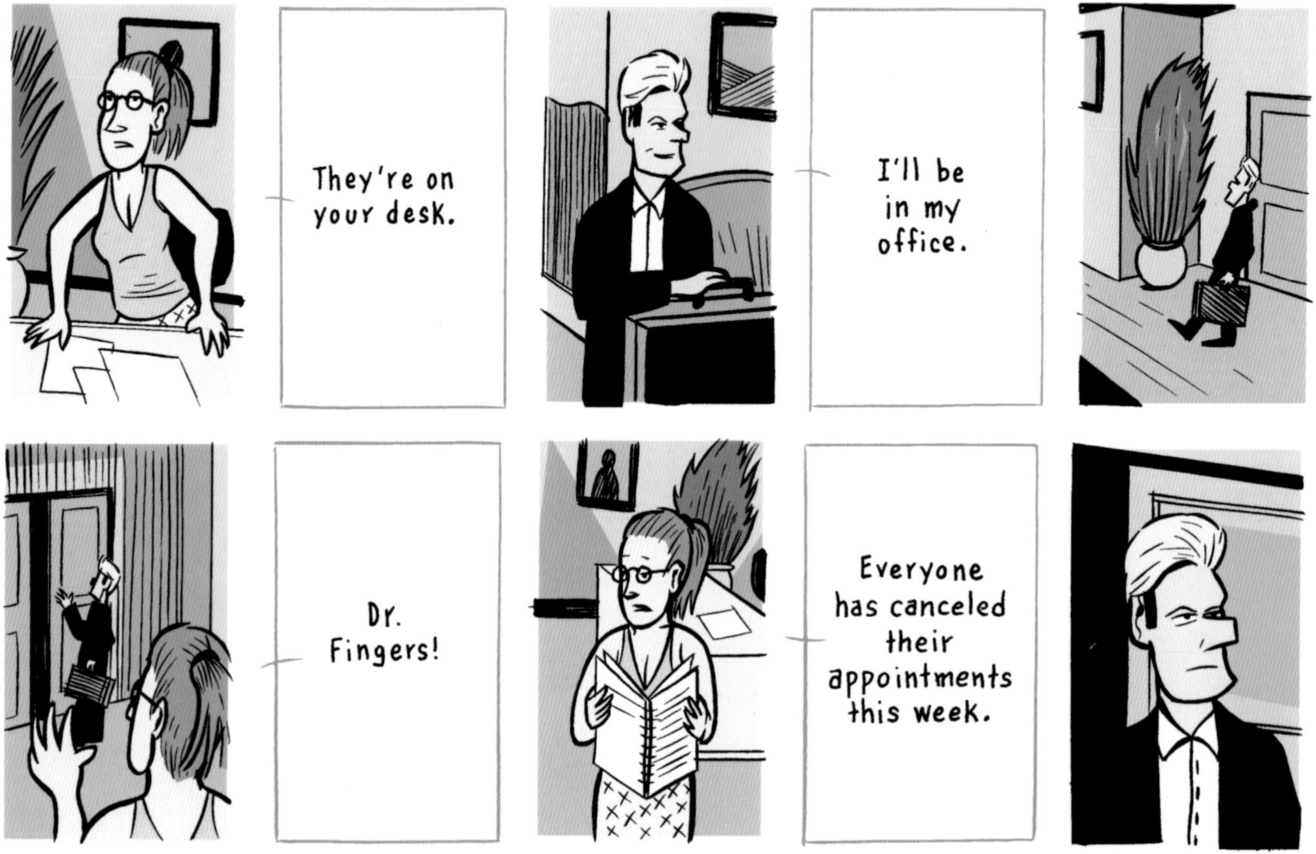
They're on your desk.
I'll be in my office.
Dr. Fingers!
Everyone has canceled their appointments this week.

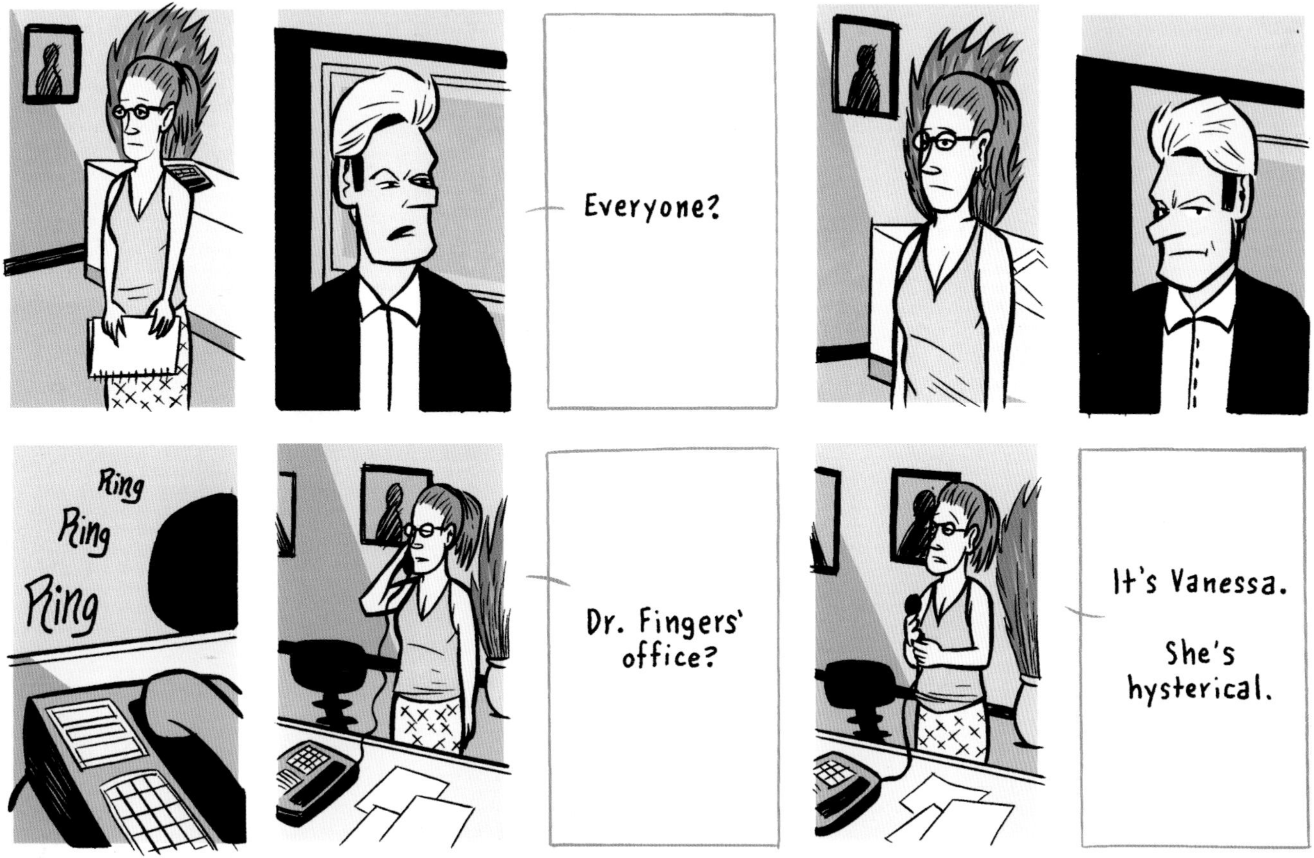
Everyone?
Ring
Ring
Ring
Dr. Fingers' office?
It's Vanessa.
She's hysterical.

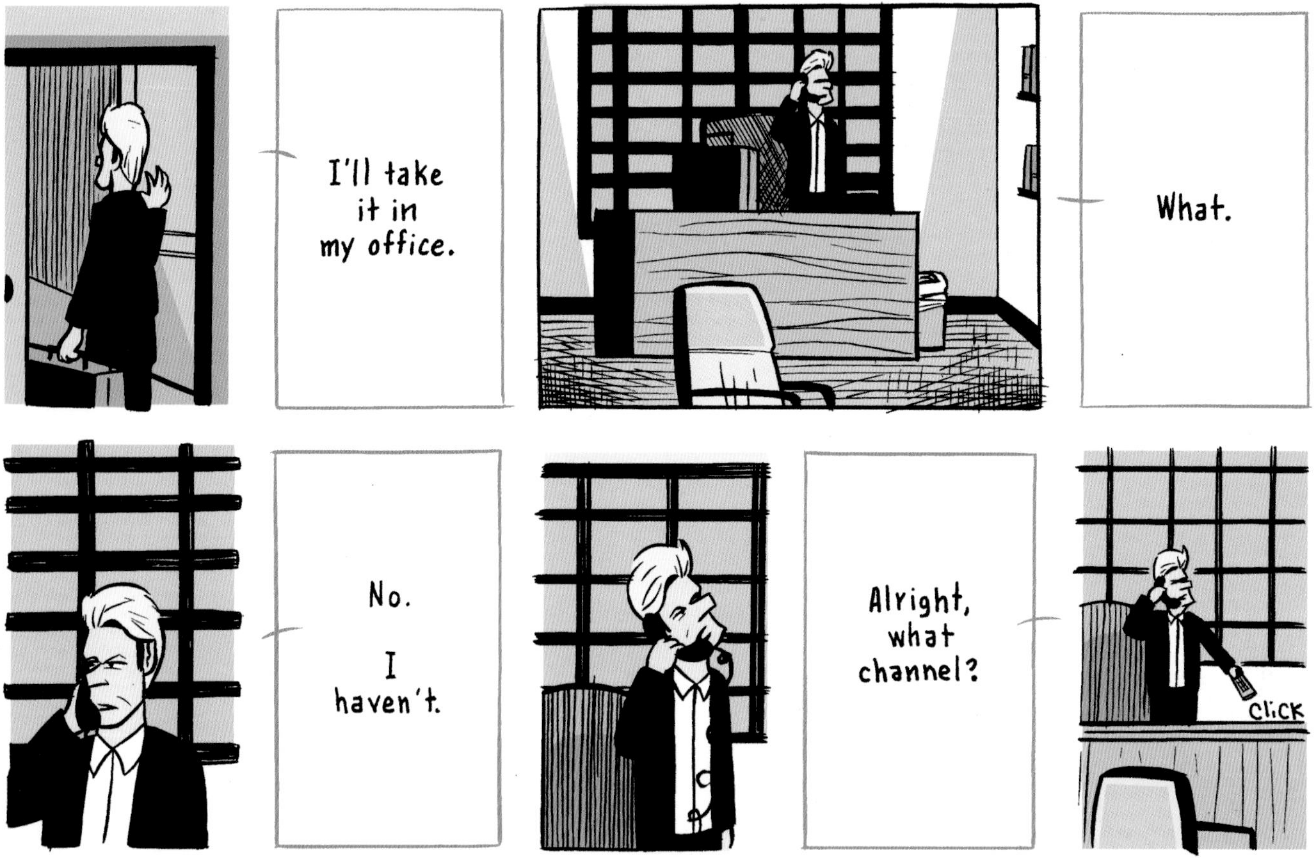
I'll take it in my office.
What.
No.
I haven't.
Alright, what channel?
CLICK

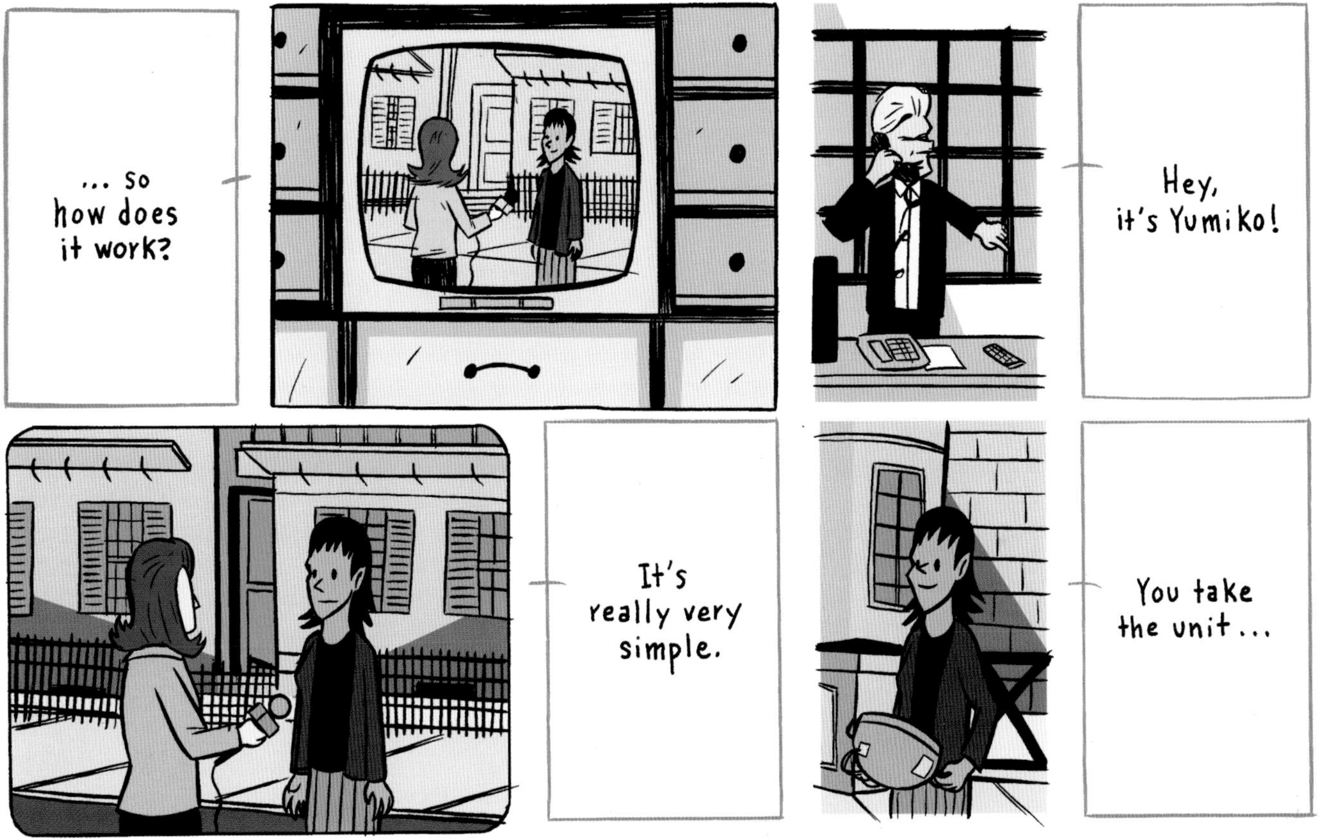
... so how does it work?
Hey, it's Yumiko!
It's really very simple.
You take the unit...

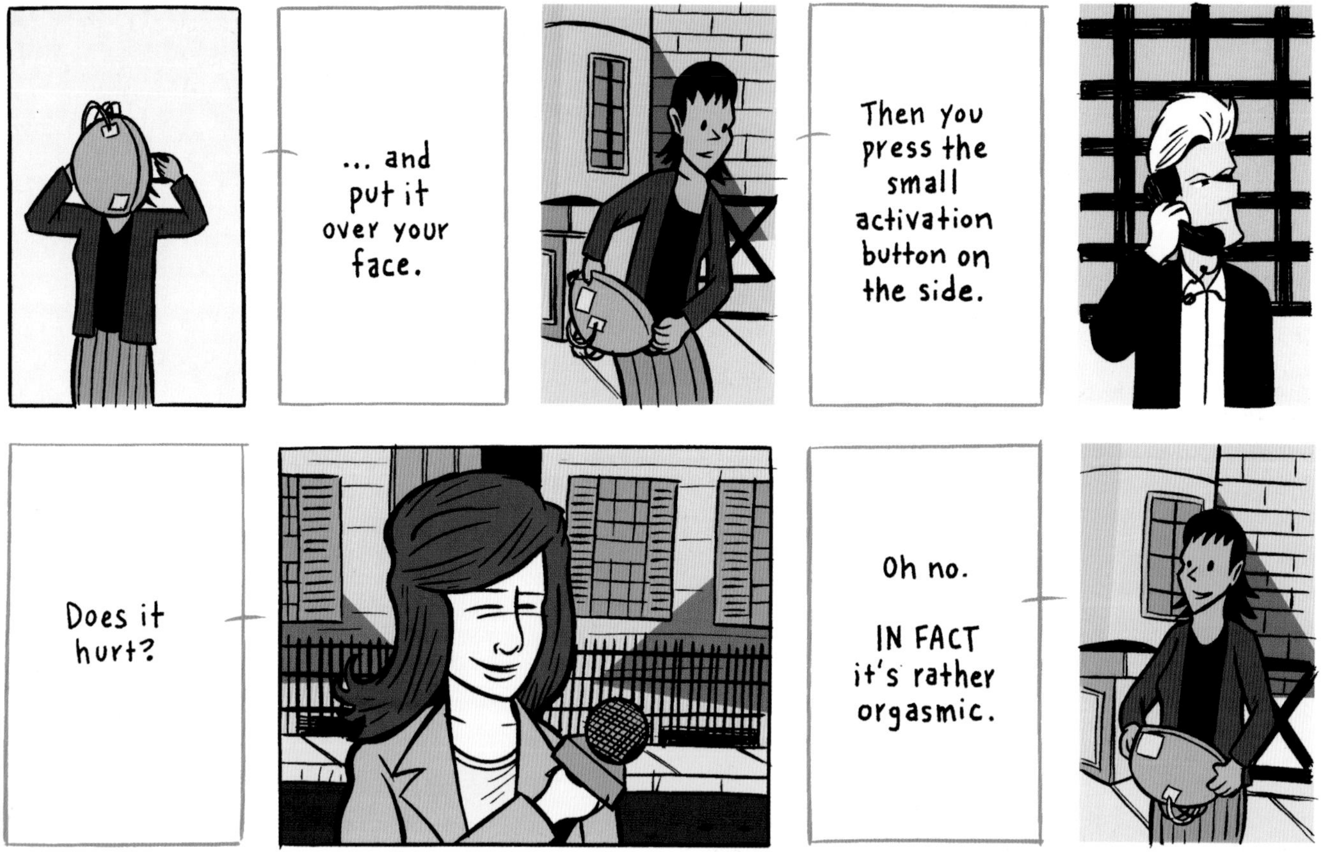
... and put it over your face.
Then you press the small activation button on the side.
Does it hurt?
Oh no.
IN FACT it's rather orgasmic.

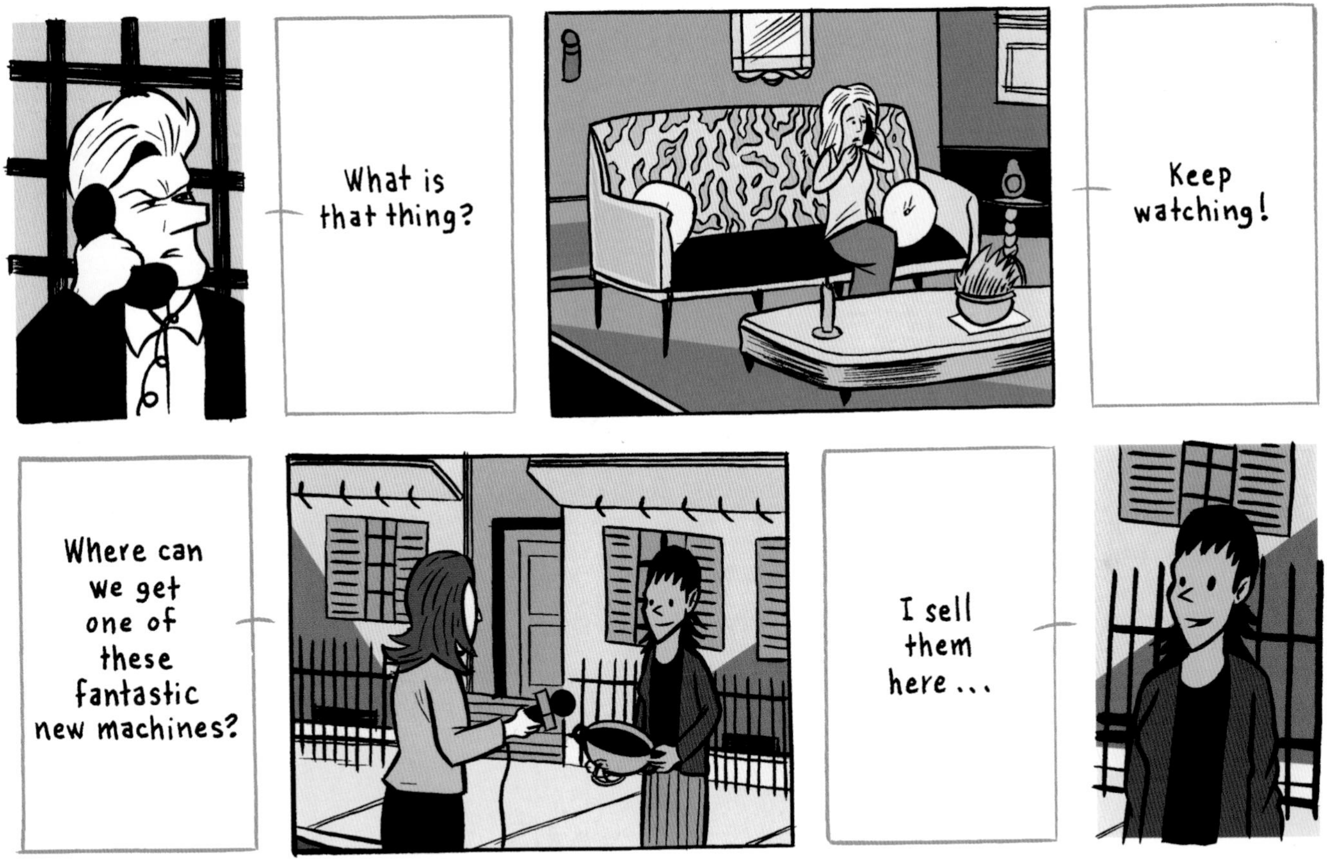
What is that thing?
Keep watching!
Where can we get one of these fantastic new machines?
I sell them here ...

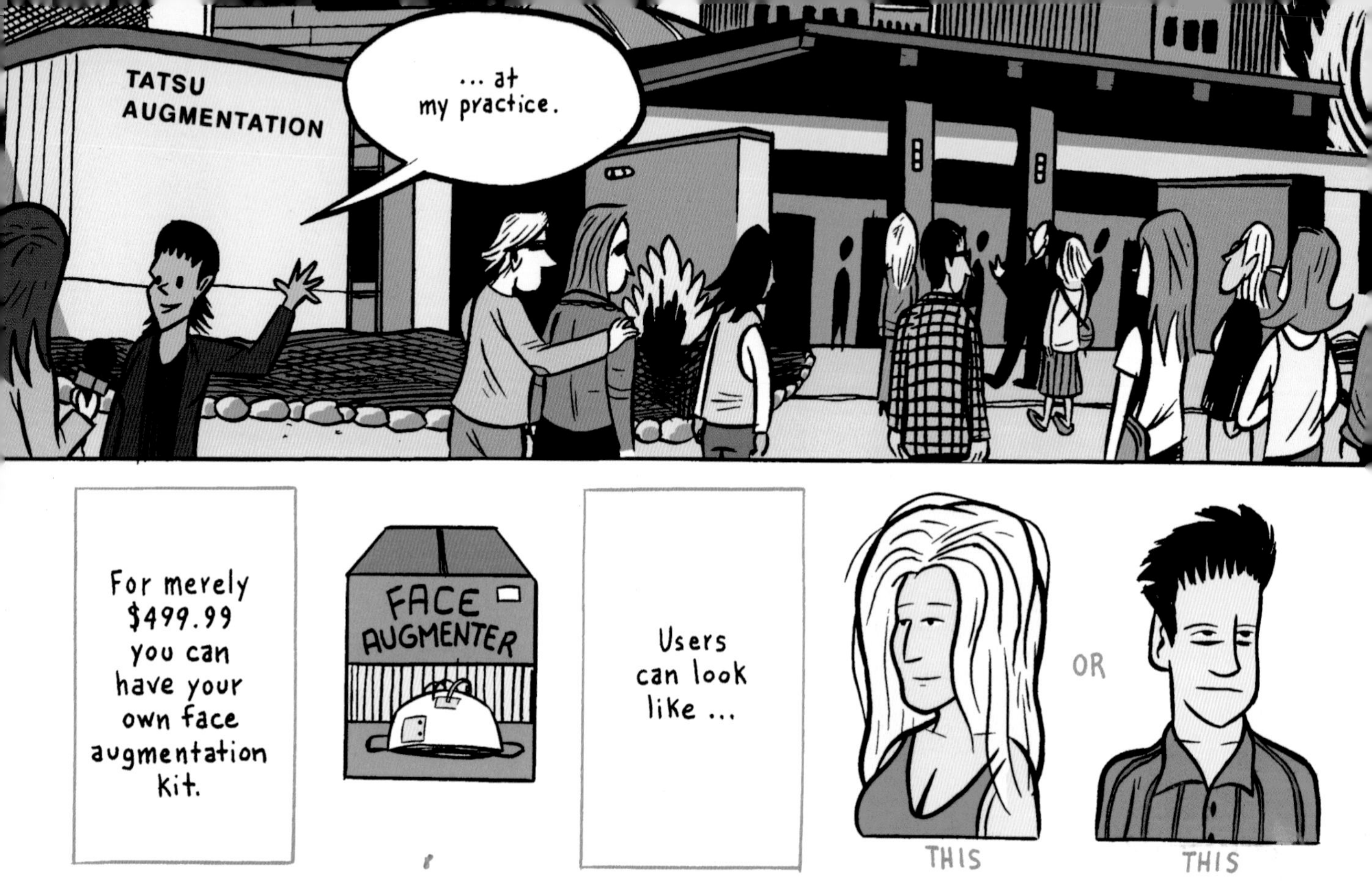
TATSU AUGMENTATION
... at my practice.
For merely $499.99 you can have your own face augmentation kit.
FACE AUGMENTER
Users can look like ...
THIS
OR
THIS

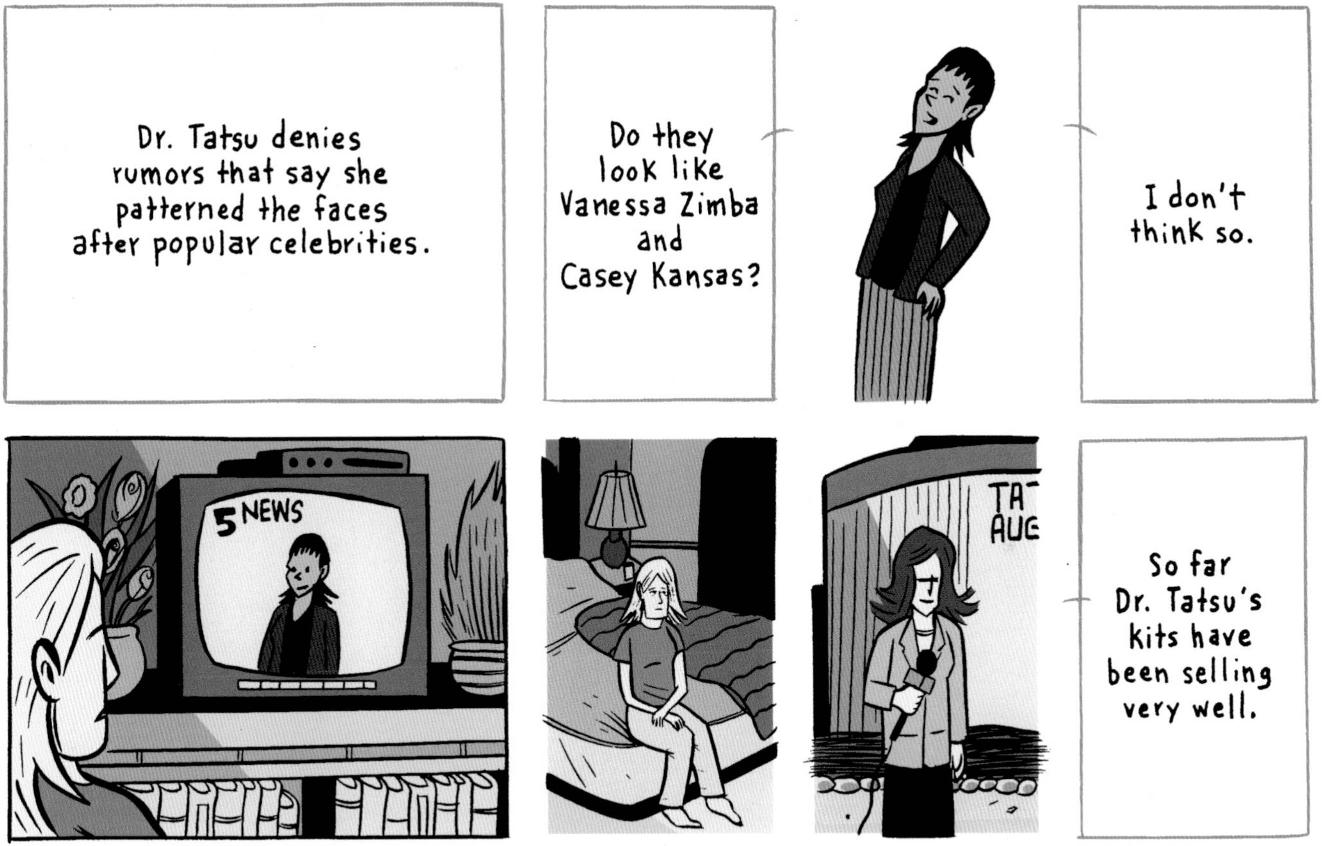
Dr. Tatsu denies rumors that say she patterned the faces after popular celebrities.
Do they look like Vanessa Zimba and Casey Kansas?
I don't think so.
5 NEWS
TA
AUG
So far Dr. Tatsu's kits have been selling very well.

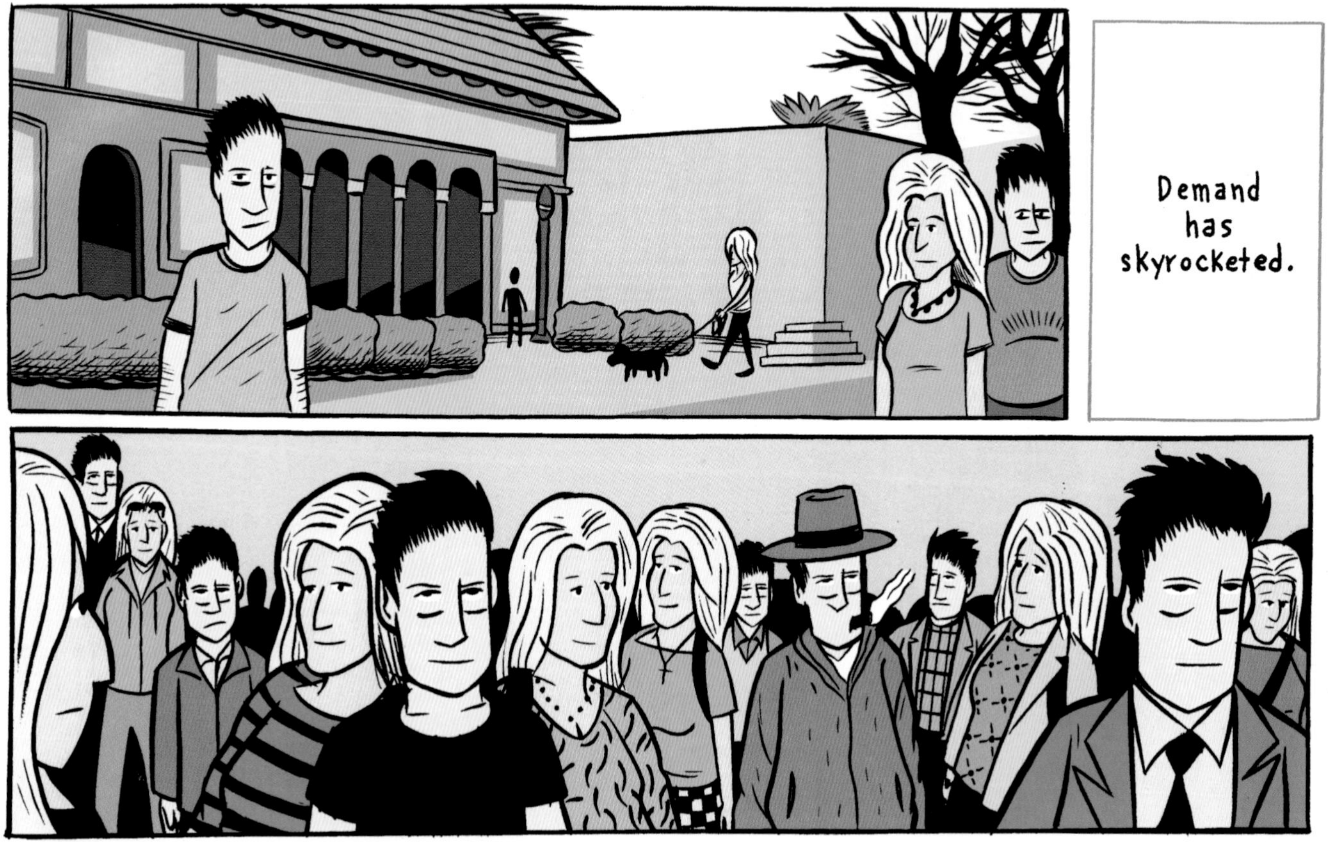
Demand has skyrocketed.

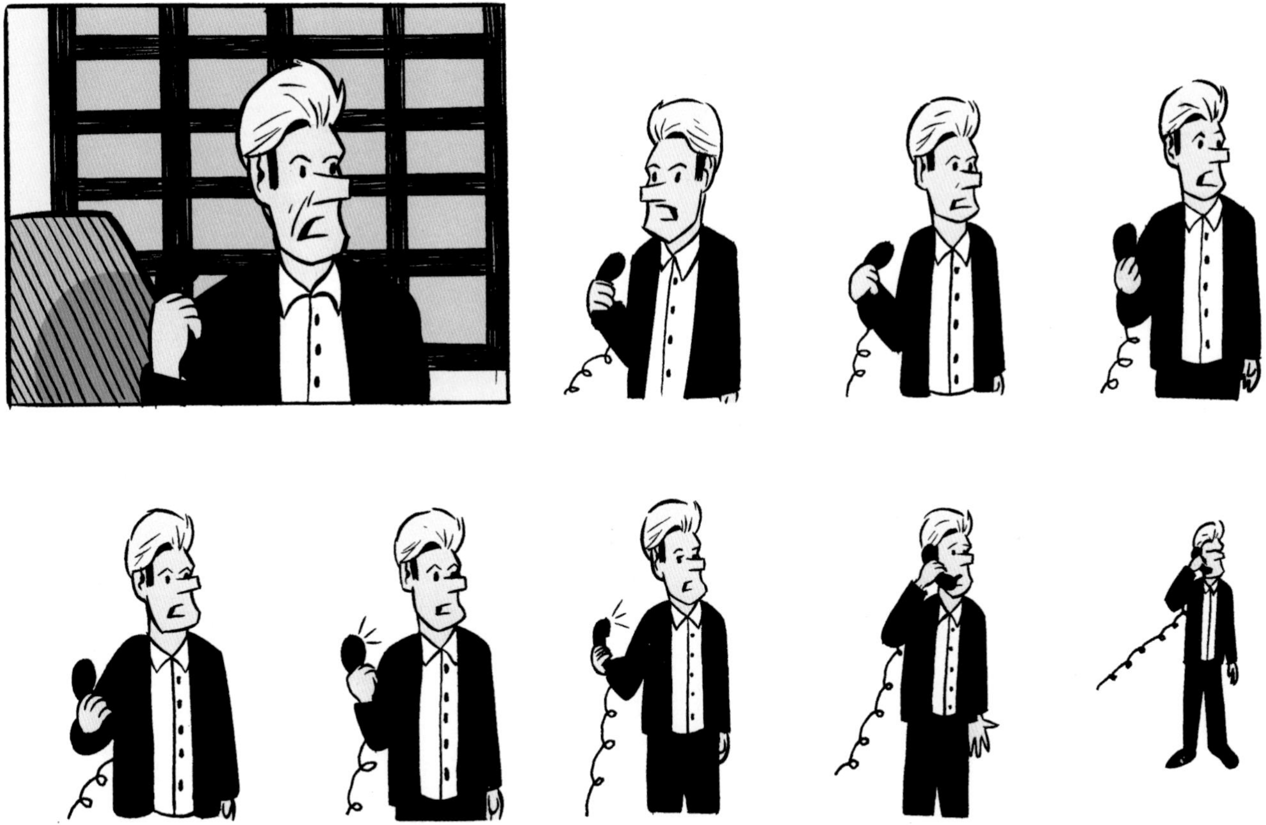

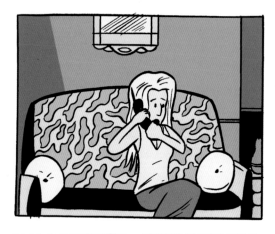

Meet me
at Casey's
house.
I'm worried.

He won't
answer his
phone.

68

Casey!

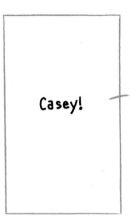
Casey!

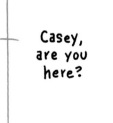
Casey, are you here?

Fingers!

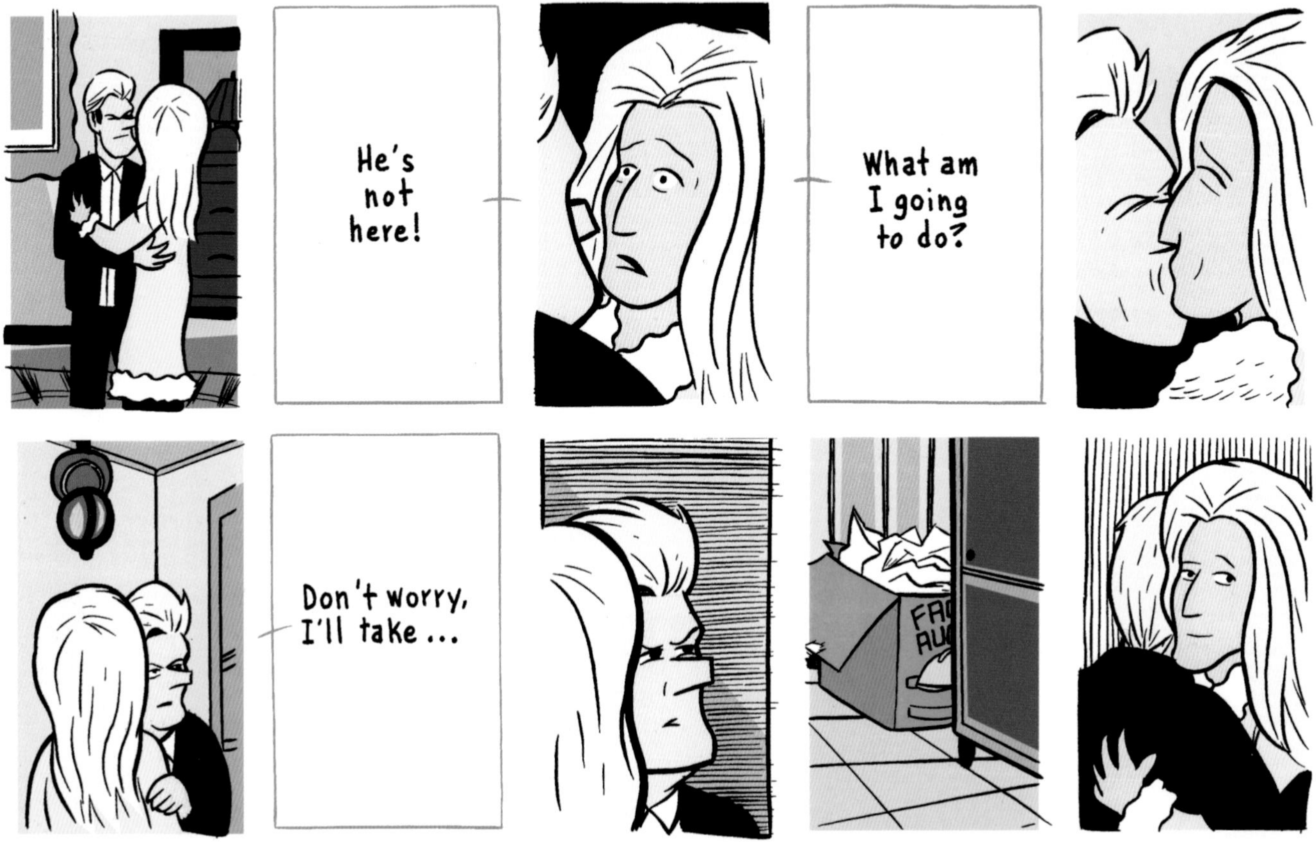
He's not here!
What am I going to do?
Don't worry, I'll take...

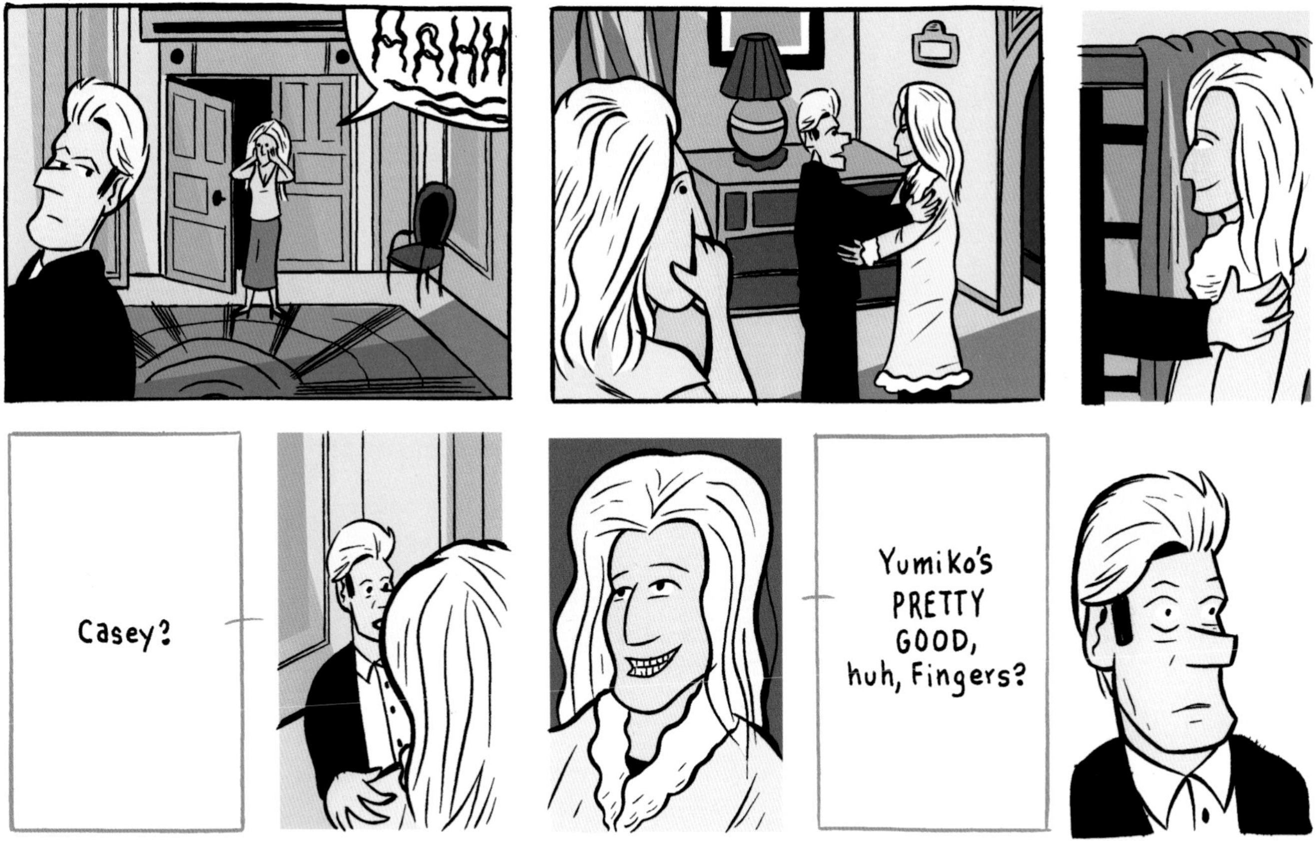
HAHH
Casey?
Yumiko's PRETTY GOOD, huh, Fingers?

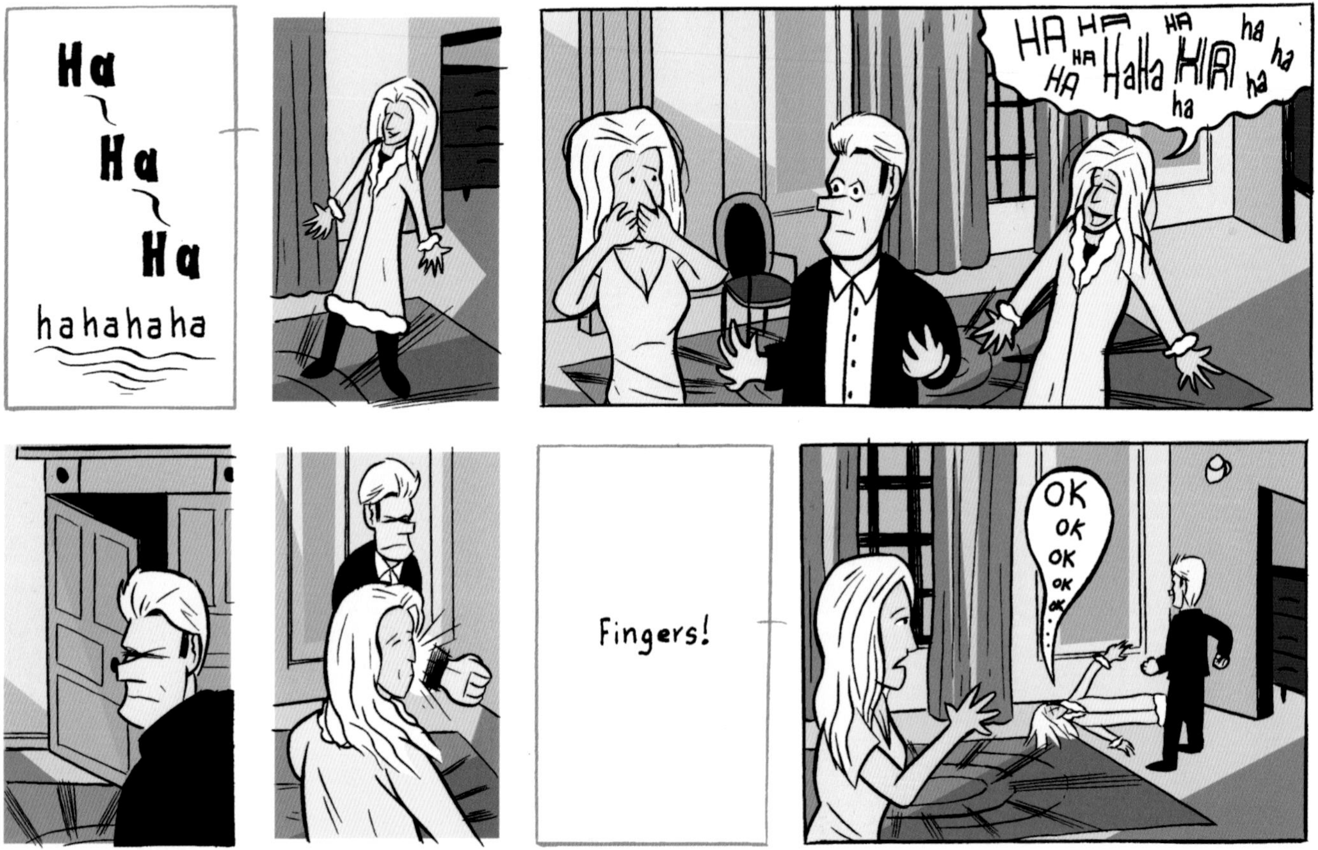

Ha
Ha
Ha
hahahaha
HA HA HA HA HA HaHa HA HA ha ha ha ha ha
Fingers!
OK OK OK OK OK

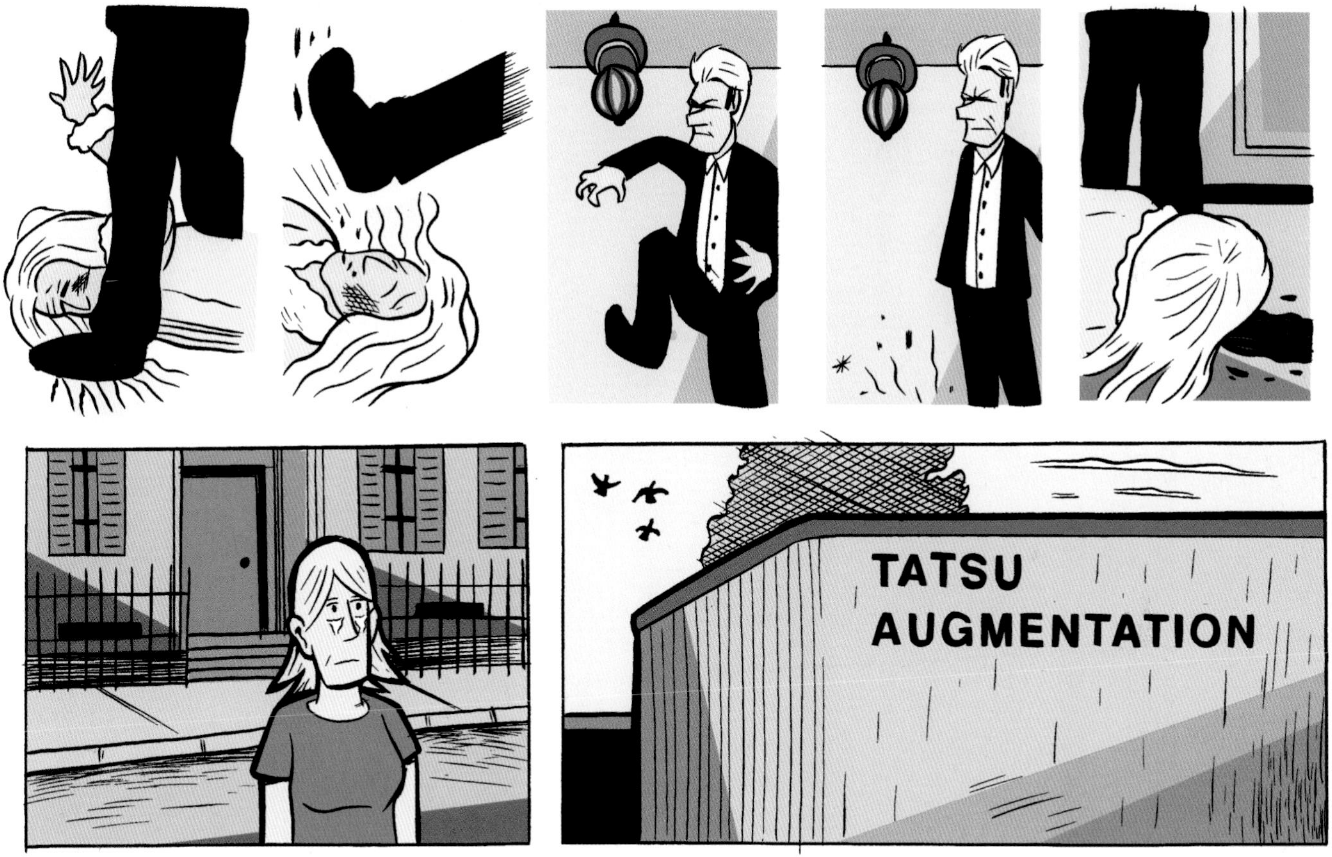
TATSU
AUGMENTATION

74

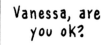

Vanessa, are you ok?

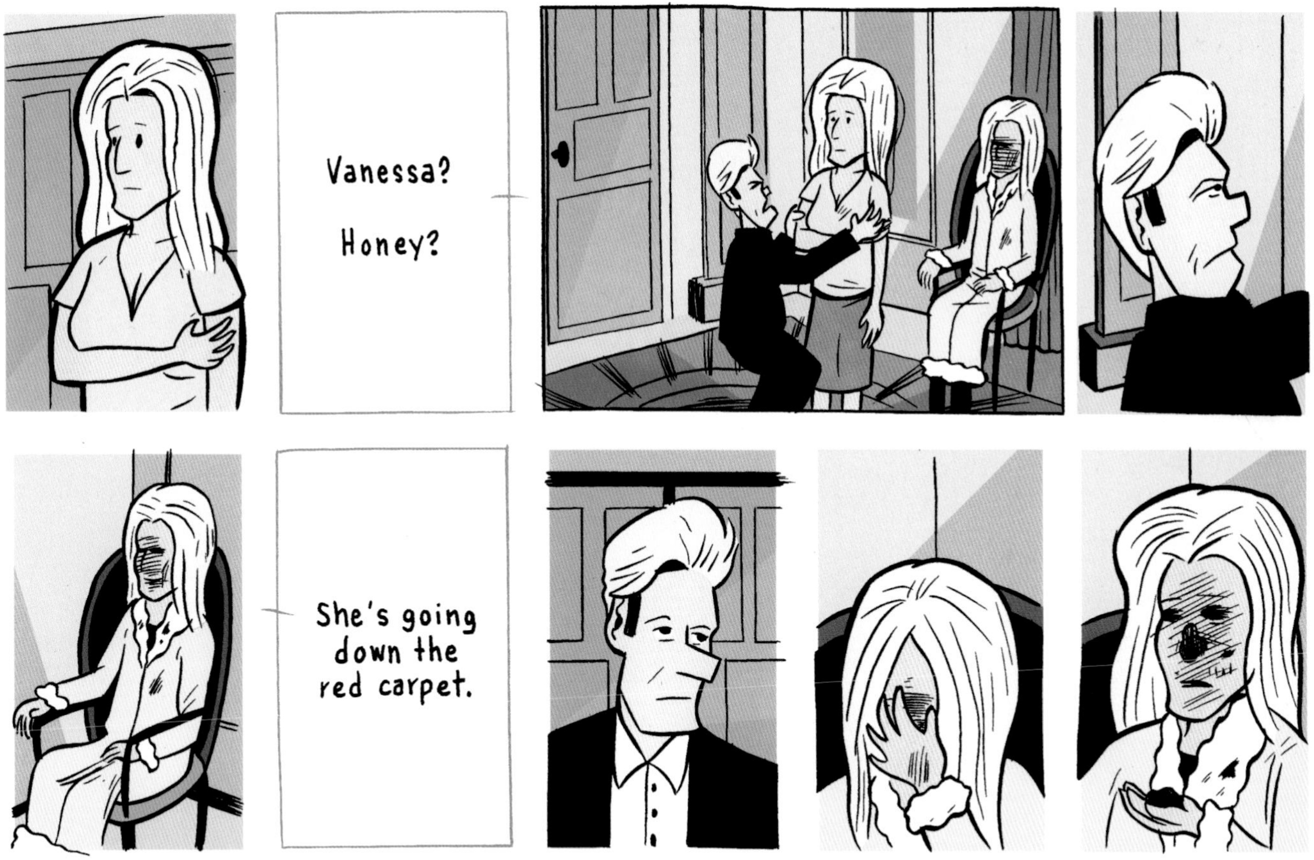
Vanessa?
Honey?
She's going down the red carpet.

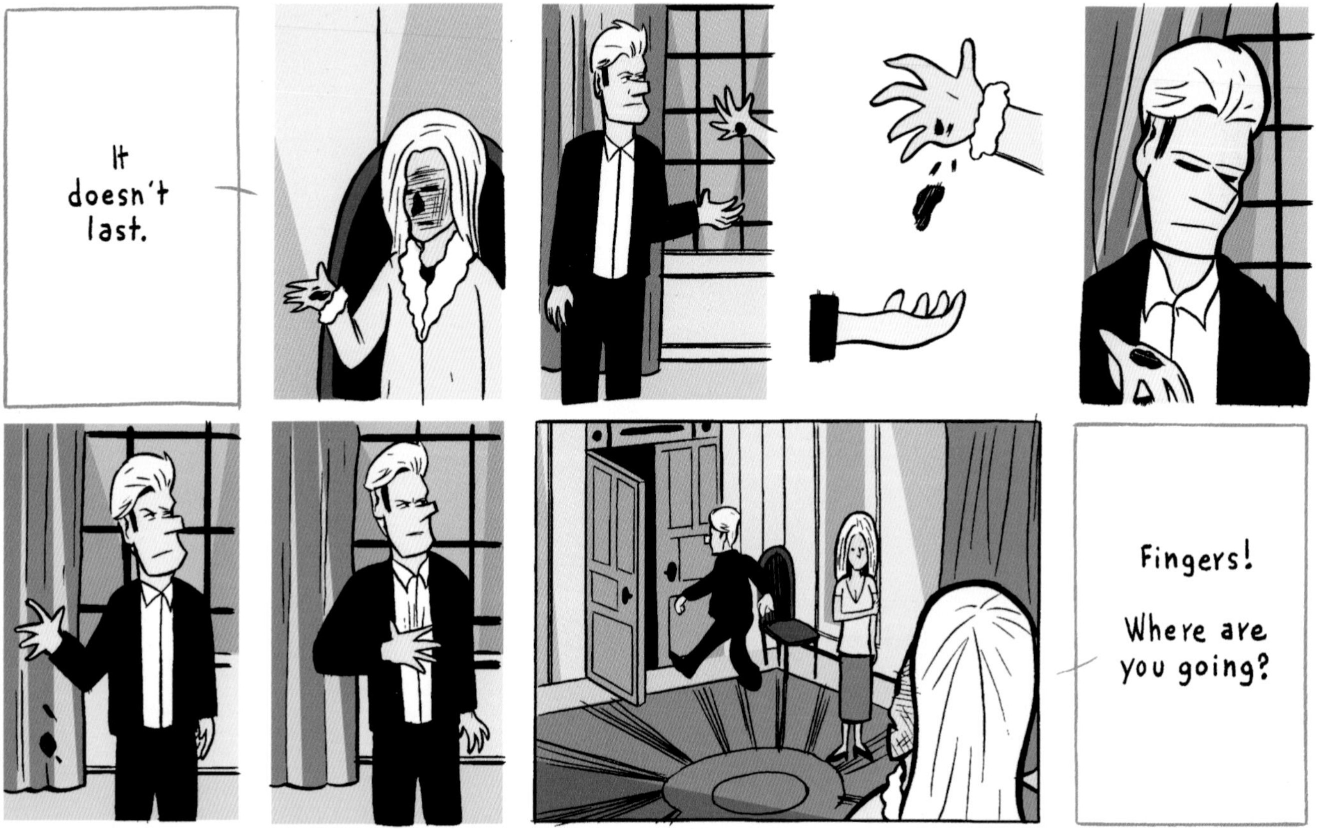
It doesn't last.
Fingers!
Where are you going?

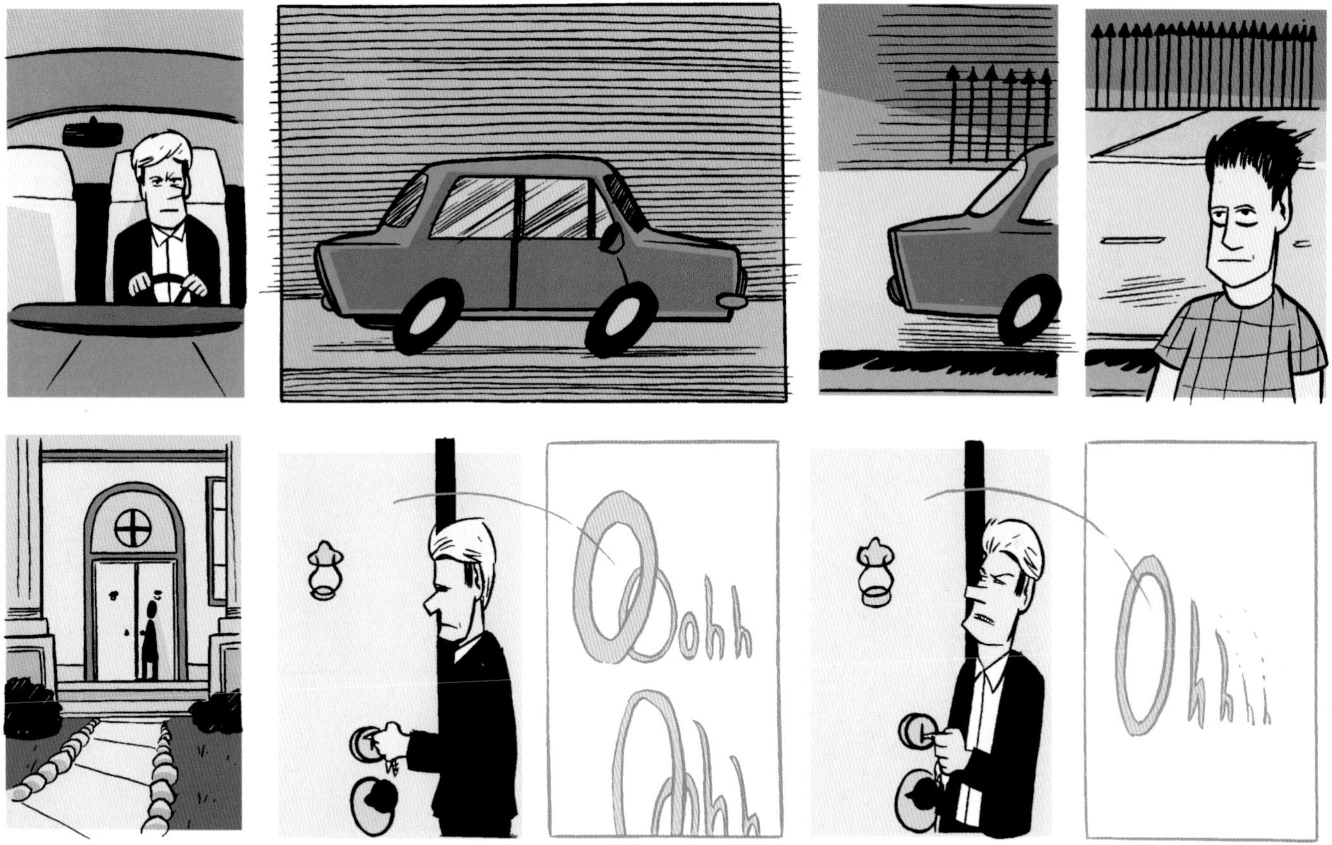
Oohh
Oohh
Ohhh

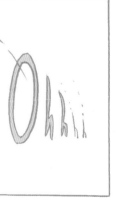

gasp
Jennifer?

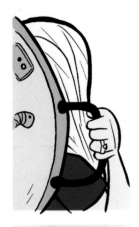

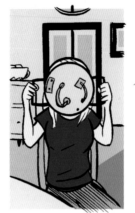

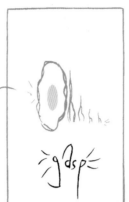

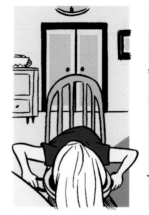

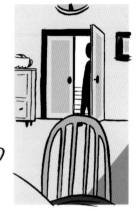

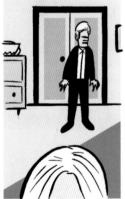

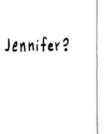

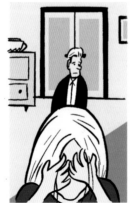

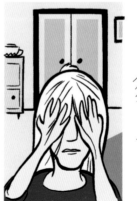

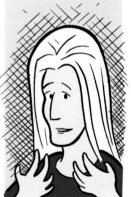

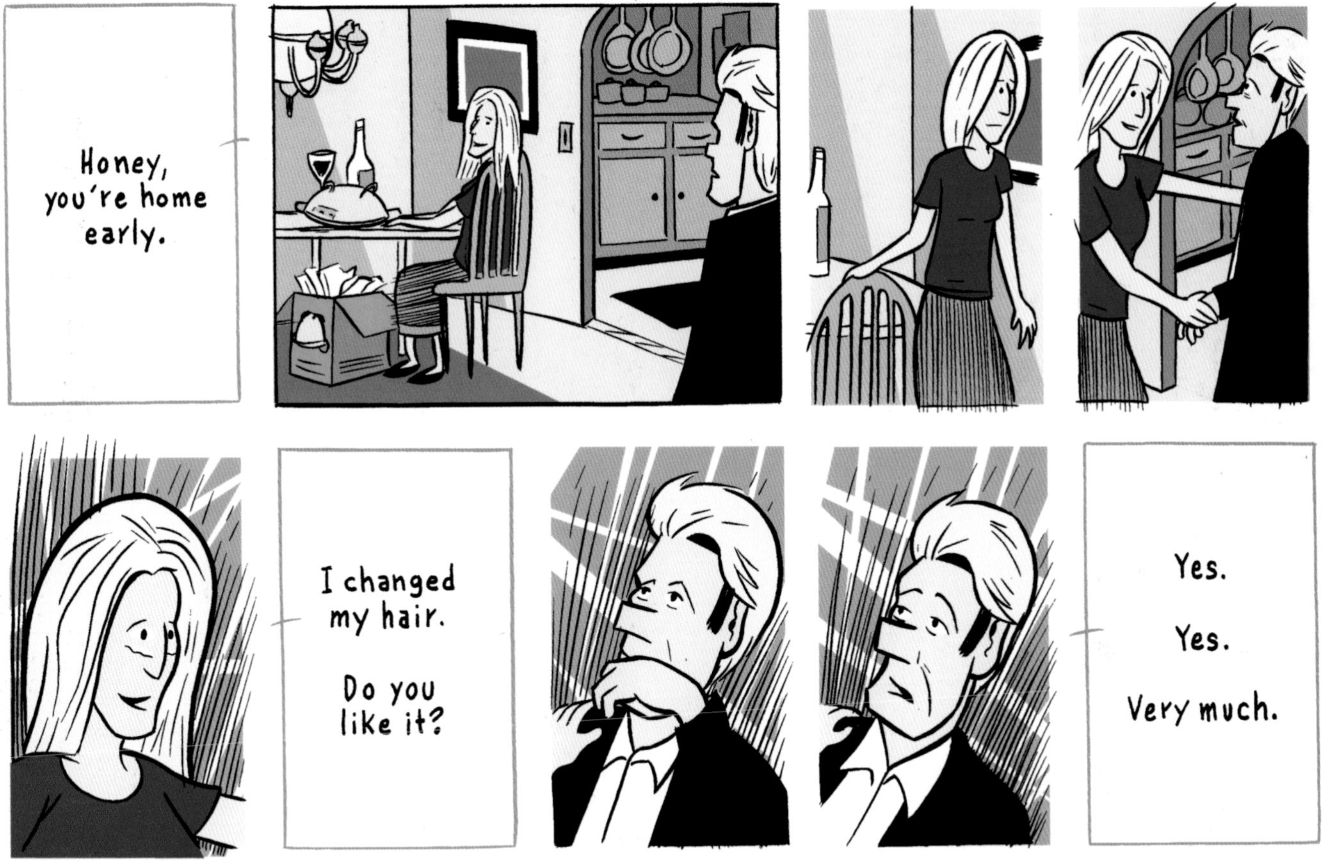
Honey, you're home early.
I changed my hair.
Do you like it?
Yes.
Yes.
Very much.

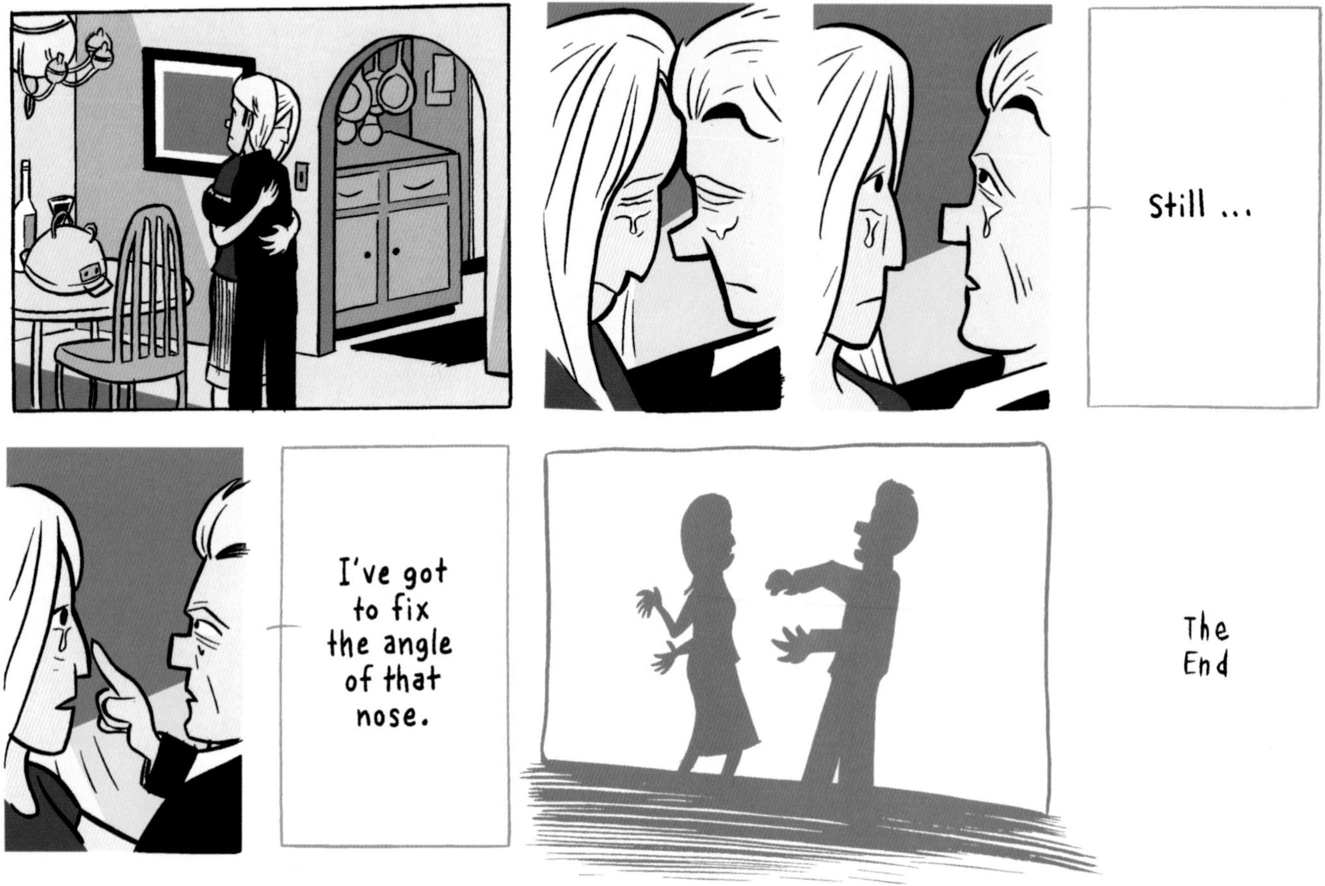
Still ...
I've got to fix the angle of that nose.
The End

EPILOGUE

Cher
THUD
Thud
Thud
THUD
303
We have to leave.
Hey!
What's the hurry?

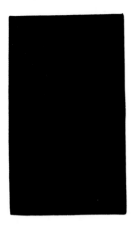

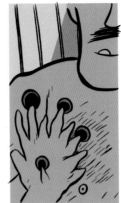

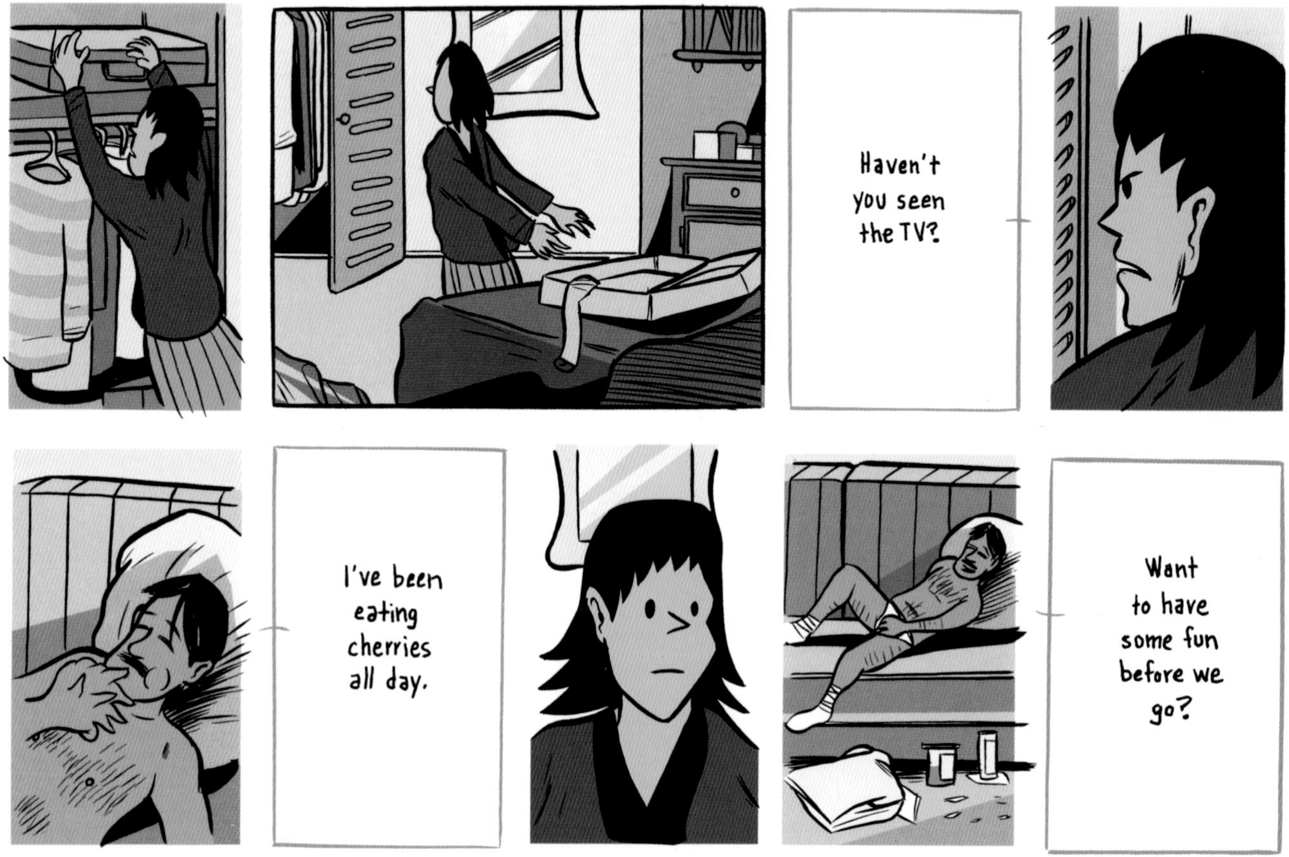
Haven't you seen the TV?
I've been eating cherries all day.
Want to have some fun before we go?

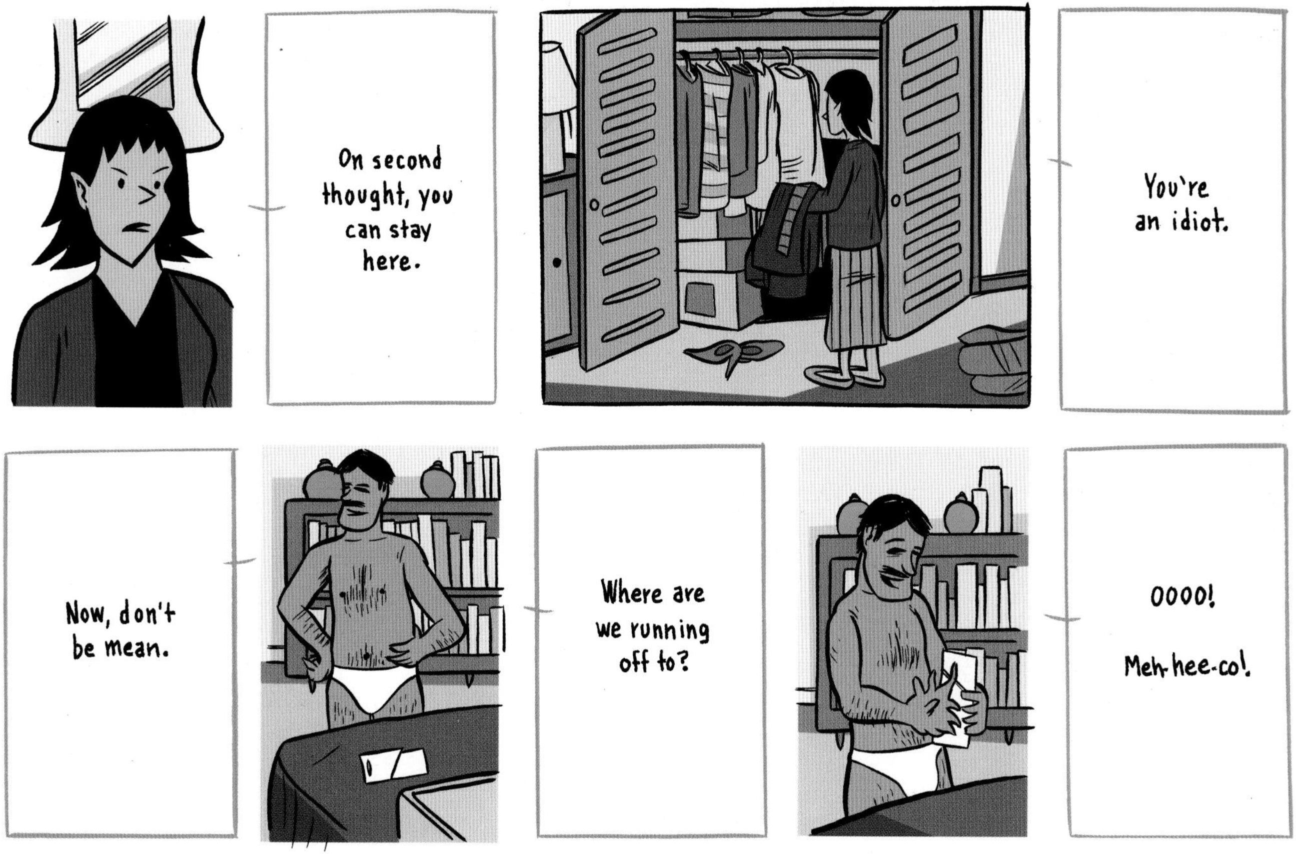
On second thought, you can stay here.
You're an idiot.
Now, don't be mean.
Where are we running off to?
OOOO!
Meh-hee-co!

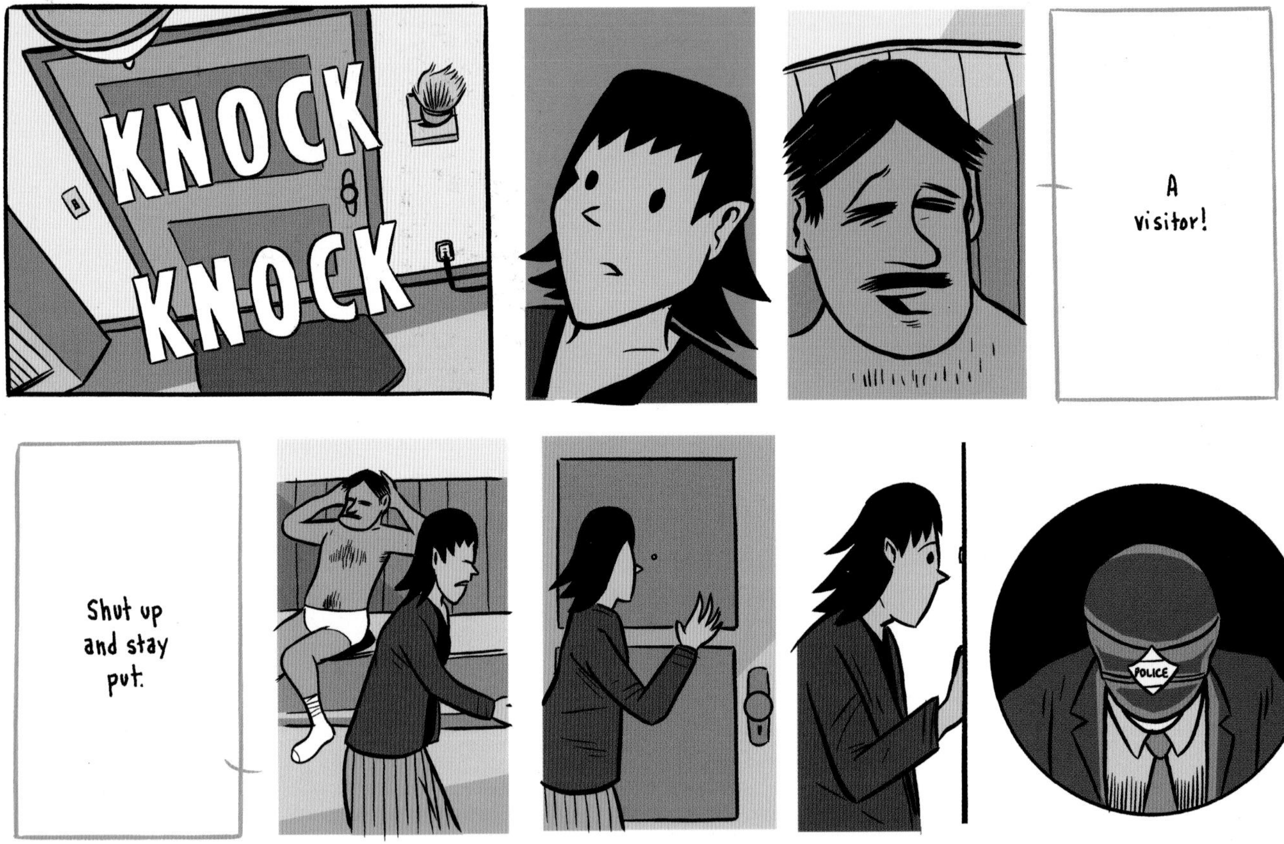
KNOCK KNOCK
A visitor!
Shut up and stay put.
POLICE

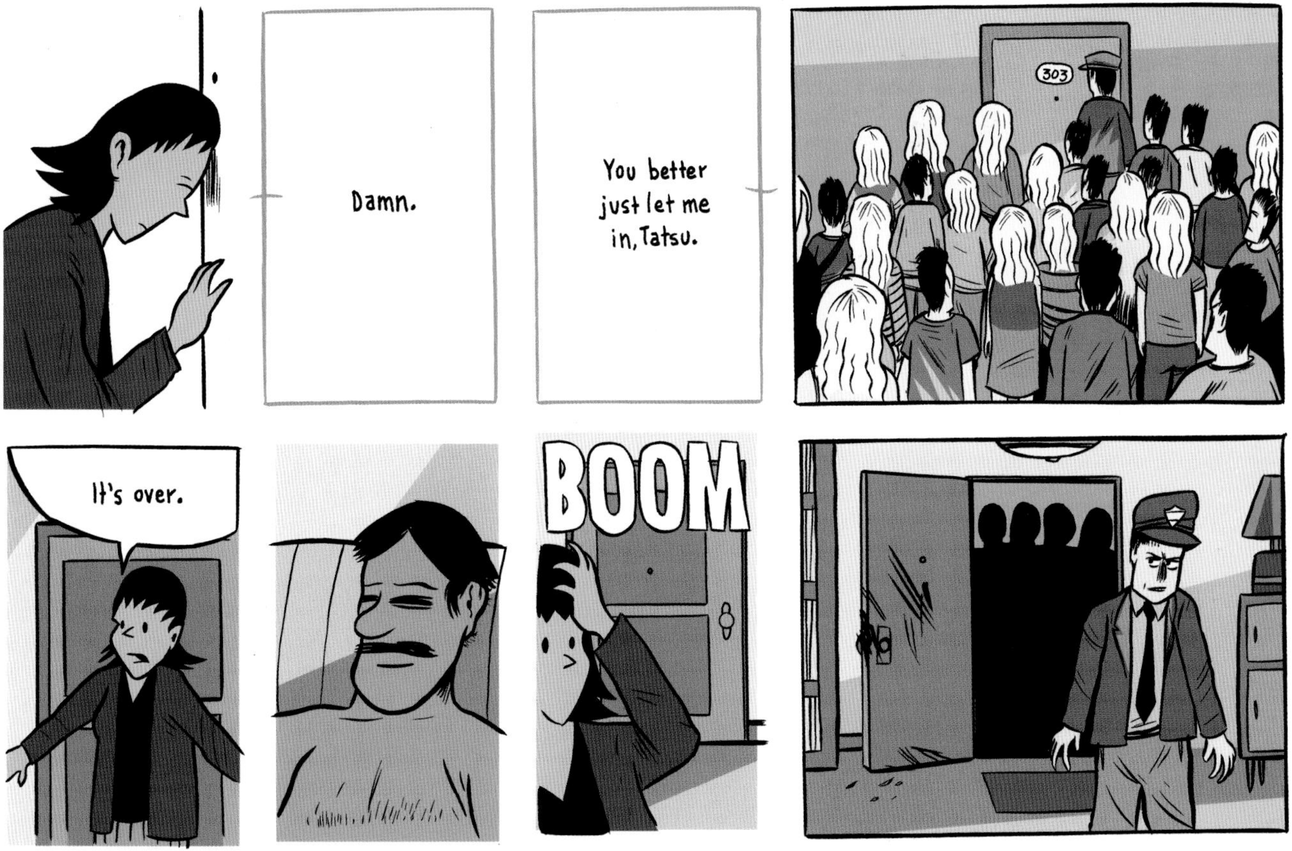
Damn.
You better just let me in, Tatsu.
303
It's over.
BOOM

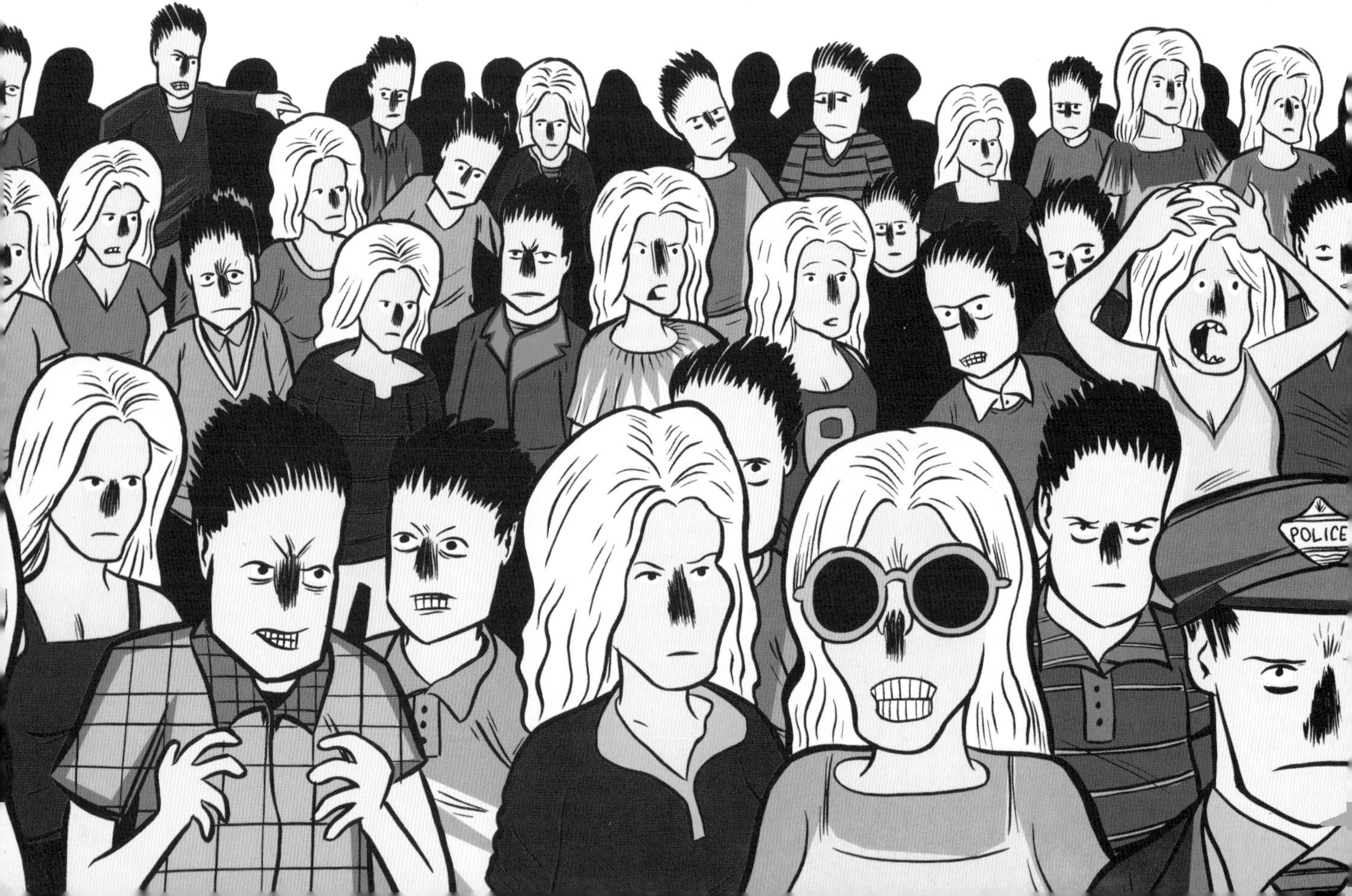
POLICE

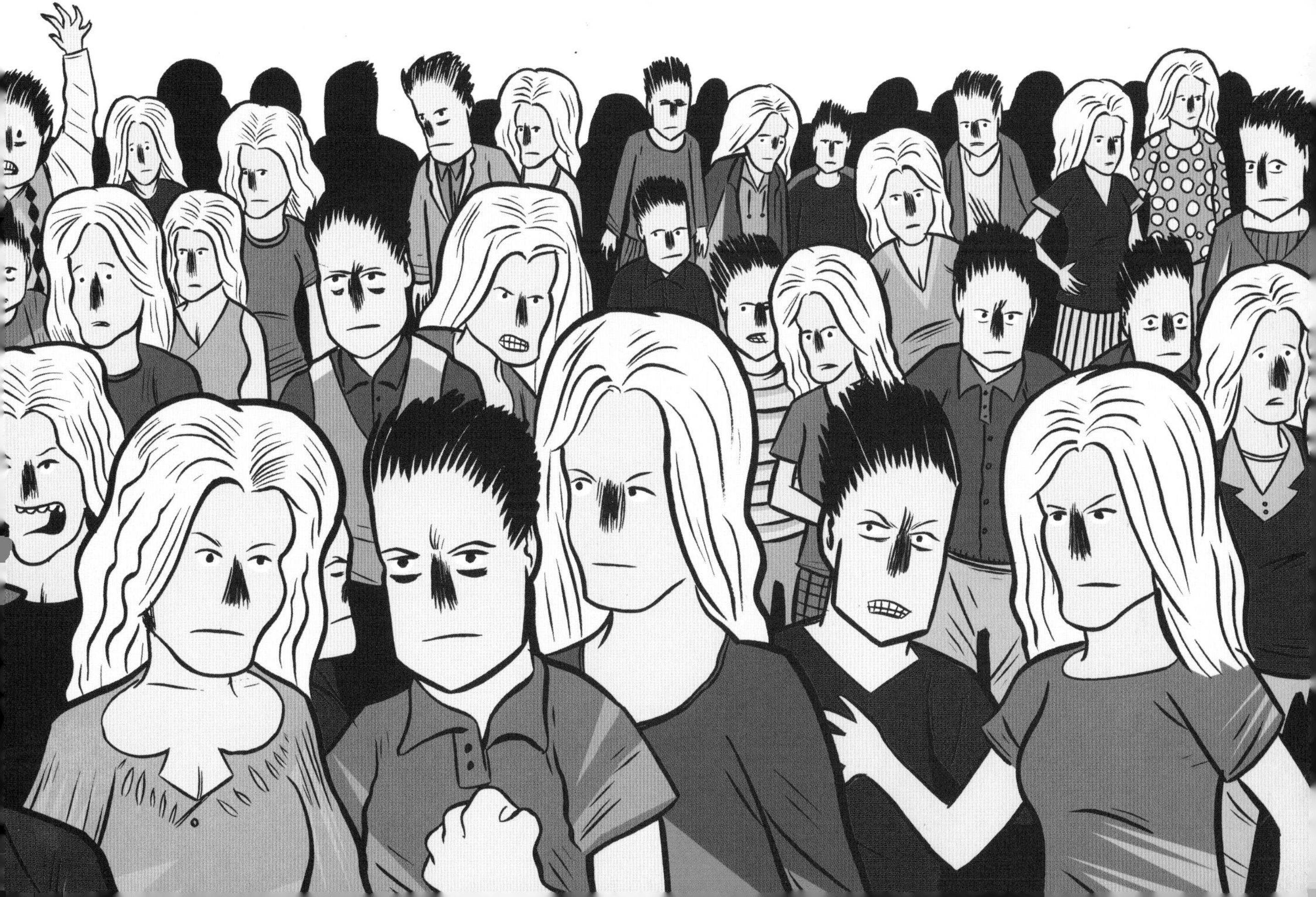

THANK
YOU

PEOPLE Brett Warnock, Chris Staros, Sarah Morean, Pat Callahan, Jody Williams, Vincent Stall

PLACES The American Red Cross, TLG, That Dunn Bros. in St. Paul, Butter, The Spy House

THINGS Laptop computer, Winsor Newton Series 7 Brush, Wacom Tablet

INSPIRATION Robert Heinlein, F. Scott Fitzgerald, Celebrity Blogs, *Flesh Wounds* by Virginia L. Blum, "Do You Think You're Beautiful?" by the Dance Hall Crashers, *Ways of Seeing* by John Berger

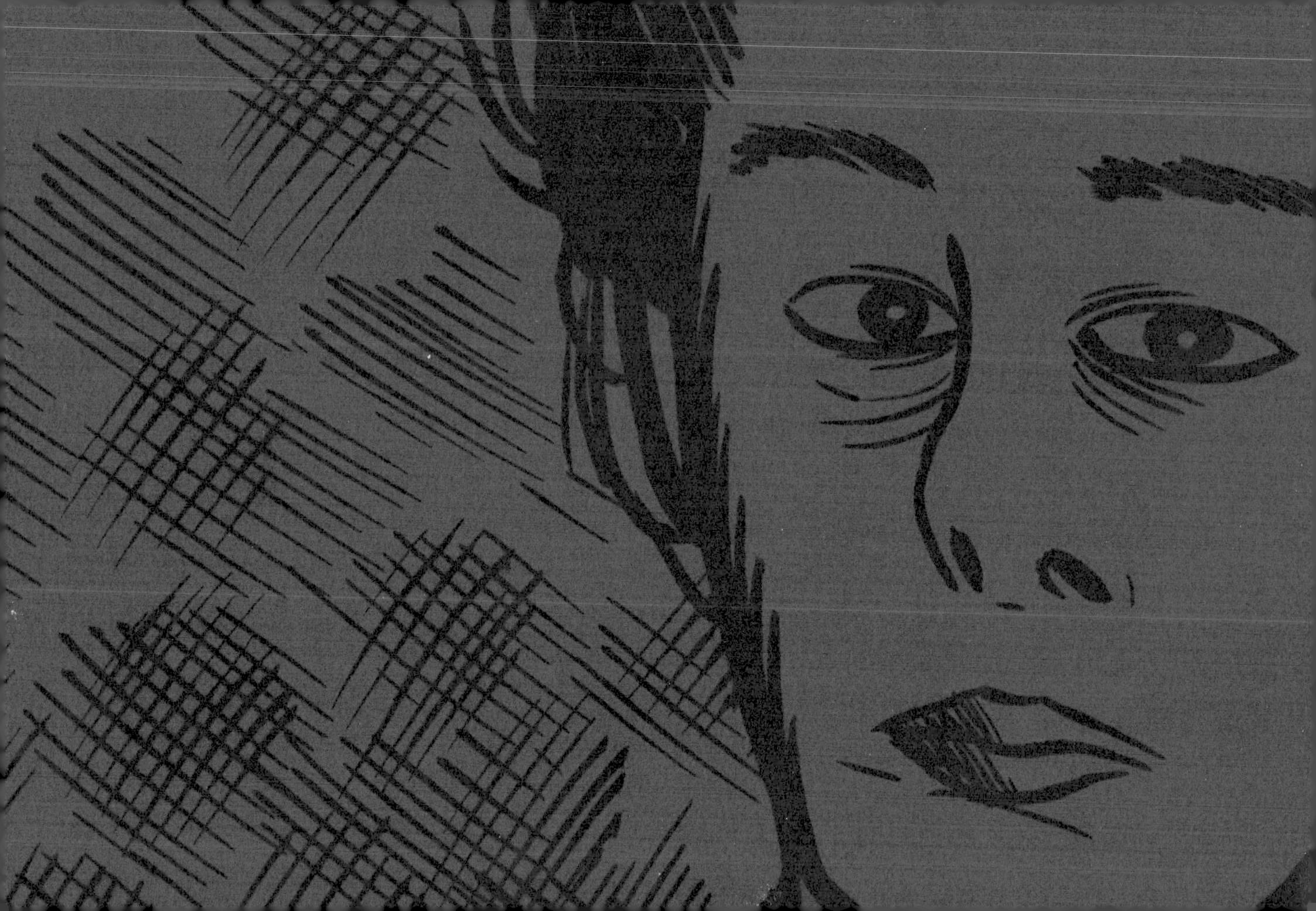